ABOUT THE AUTHOR

Grey Wolf is a Lakota who grew up in a rural North American community under the guidance of his grandfather, the community's Holy Man. He currently teaches the traditions of his people in schools, colleges and workshop groups. He is the primary author of *Earth Signs* and *The Friendship Pack*.

DEDICATION

I dedicate this book to my wife, Rachel. She has done a great deal to help in the writing of this book by putting up with the long periods of time that I hide in my office, lost in the morass of a temperamental computer. More than that, her curiosity about her own Native roots inspired the quest for knowledge which led to this book.

NATIVE AMERICAN WISDOM

Piatkus Guides

Other titles in this series include

PIATKUS GUIDES

NATIVE AMERICAN WISDOM

Grey Wolf

PIATKUS

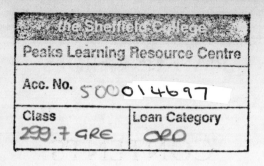
Neither the author nor the publisher is responsible for any harm caused to anyone undertaking the exercises and meditations in this book. Anyone who has suffered from a mental or emotional illness should seek medical advice before attempting the exercises.

© 2000 by Grey Wolf

First published in 2000 by
Judy Piatkus (Publishers) Ltd
5 Windmill Street
London W1P 1HF
e-mail: info@piatkus.co.uk

For the latest news and information on all our titles, visit
our website at www.piatkus.co.uk

The moral rights of the author have been asserted
A catalogue record for this book is available from the British Library

ISBN 0-7499-2065-3

Design by Paul Saunders
Edited by Rachel Connolly

Typeset by Action Publishing Technology Ltd., Gloucester
Printed and bound in Great Britain by
Mackays of Chatham PLC

CONTENTS

PROLOGUE

I would like to take this opportunity to clarify two points. The first is to make clear my definitions of a Native American and a New American. You need to be aware of the misunderstanding that is common in the identification of America as a Nation. On the continent of North America there are three major countries: Canada, Mexico and the United States of America. Due to the length of its name most people refer to the United States by the abbreviated name, America. Yet in this book, I refer to Native Americans as the descendants of the Nations of the continents that existed prior to the invention of such countries as Canada or the United States. I refer to the New Americans as those people who are not of indigenous ancestry, those that have arrived from other lands, and their descendants. I state this now so that you will not be distracted or confused when I fail to identify a difference between a Native group that is in or from Canada and those in or from the United States.

Secondly, and most importantly, it must be understood that I do not speak for all Native Americans. I can only tell you of things as I perceive them. Even points of historical context are subject to interpretation by each individual that examines them. So, in reading this work you may find interpretations of things that others would dispute. That does not make either party wrong – just different. Each individual finds their own truths based on their experiences and belief in what they are taught. What follows is an account of some of the truths as I perceive them at this time.

INTRODUCTION

In *Black Elk Speaks* John Neihardt transcribed the account of the life of the Lakota Holy Man, Nicholas Black Elk. At one point in this account Black Elk says that the 'hoop of the Nation is broken'. He was speaking of the Lakota as a collective of people that had lived a way of life that it would never be possible to return to.

This can be said of every culture, civilisation and age that humans have been involved in since the dawn of creation. We still spend a great deal of our time harking back to the way things were. People of the modern world, with its high technology, fast pace and ever increasing feelings of loss of independence and direction, are a people whose hoops have been broken.

Many individuals are now looking to 'the old ways' for guidance on a better way to live. They look at the way of the Celts, of the Orient and of the Aborigine, and quite often the way of Native Americans. In this search there has been a tendency to view Native Americans as a people residing in the past, still living in tipis and hunting buffalo. This is far from true. To begin with, very few of the Natives of North America were among the nomadic hunters and gatherers of the high plains, most were stationary and involved in an agricultural form of lifestyle. The romantic image of Native America is largely a product of Hollywood imagery.

There is, however, a valid reason to look to Native American culture and spirituality as a guide for today's life. As is the case of all peoples in their past, Native Americans looked to and lived closely with the Mother Earth and the rest of the natural world around them. This includes all the varieties of peoples of Native America. Their 'primitive' philosophy and spirituality was the one thing they held in common, irrespective of their differences. This holds true right to this day. Our culture and spirituality are still holding our individual hoops together, and helping us to repair the hoops of our Nations and to form the new hoops that will allow us to develop personally and collectively for the future.

In addition to helping us, the gifts of our traditions can be of help to people of any culture, as they can be used to aid in the recovery and repair of the hoop of any person.

I hope to help the readers of this book to sift through the morass of romantic imagery of Native America and to find the truths that are available for all to take on and use for themselves.

In the way that I work and teach I base everything upon

my upbringing. I was raised by my grandfather, the Holy Man of a relocated community, and taught in the old ways in so far as they were relevant to life in 20th-century Western civilisation. I practised my spirituality with the aid of the Sweatlodge, from the age of seven, went through crying for a vision in my early teens, and a rite of passage to teach me about becoming a man at sixteen. All these events are part of my foundation, but as with all things of life my beginnings are not the end of my growth. I have continued to seek spiritual strength and wisdom throughout my life in a way that has led me to a more complete connection with Mother Earth and *Mitakuye Oyasin* (all my relations).

Over the course of the book you will get a taste of the things mentioned here in a way that will allow you to take into your own life those elements that you find to be helpful for your growth and development. I have never given a talk or led a workshop in which everyone present found that they could agree with or make use of everything that was presented to them. I expect the same will hold true for the readers of this work. Not everything that follows will be for everyone that reads it, but everyone will find something of personal value if they just open their hearts and receive the contents in the spirit in which they are offered.

I will also help the reader to gain a better understanding of Native American wisdom by presenting lessons in several ways. Among the methods will be the retelling of some stories that are used by Native Americans to help us understand, learn and enjoy the passing on of ancient wisdom. In addition, there will be details of several methods of ceremony to help you to begin bringing these lessons into practical use in your life.

The last aspect of Native American culture that I would mention here is the tools that we use in the practice of our spirituality and culture. Drums, rattles and imagery will be among those presented, along with instructions on the making of some of these items for your personal use.

I hope this text should be all anyone would need to begin a journey to a better understanding of Native America, and at the same time find something of value to take into their own lives, making it richer and more balanced.

1

MANY PEOPLES IN MANY LANDS

Most people in today's world have a very limited perception of the diversity that was/is Native America. We are visually remembered by the majority of people as the horse riding, tipi dwelling, buffalo hunters of the high plains, those savage fighters that captured poor innocent pioneer women and children after the slaughter and scalping of their peaceful, brave settler husbands and fathers.

Names such as Sitting Bull, Crazy Horse, Cochise, Geronimo, Santana and Red Cloud are well known. The ideas that spring to mind for many people when they hear these names, as well as words like Sioux, Apache, Cheyenne and Pawnee, are ones of savagery and horror.

The concept is changing, however. Indeed, within my adult life I have seen a vast change. Over the last twenty years Native Americans have gone from being 'heathen savages' to 'noble redmen' in the eyes of many people. Yet this has come about without a great deal of change in what is known about the reality and diversity of Native America. What is needed, therefore, is for people to learn more of our differences, to learn and understand more of what has been contributed by our peoples to make today's world what it is. These things must be learned before we will begin to be understood and our ancestors given their due respect.

For example, few people realise that it was the Americas that sparked a dietary revolution across Europe. Prior to contact with the Americas, the food of the average people was a variety of grass grains (wheat, barley, rye and oats), a poor diet very low in protein and other nutritional requirements commonly accepted as healthy by today's standards.

Suddenly there was a substantial increase in the level of protein through adoption of the many types of beans that began to be imported from the Americas. In addition, corn, or maize as it is more commonly known in England, had a serious impact on the European diet. Corn has for many years been fed to domestic animals and substantially increased the production of chickens, pigs and cows. As a consequence, meat, eggs and milk were also more widely available.

If you examine the growth of the European population, the lessening of the impact of disease and plagues, along with the expansion of European Nations in their colonial periods, you will find that all these things correlate directly with the alteration to their diet, and this was brought about so easily due to the agricultural developments that were the responsibility of Native Americans.

There are many other things that the Natives of the Americas have contributed to the development of the world as we know it, that have been denied to the consciousness of many peoples throughout the centuries. In the past this has been accepted, if not acceptable, but the time has come for the record to be set straight. This is not just for the benefit of Native Americans, but for all people in search of a way forward for themselves, as individuals in search of wisdom that will aid them on their life paths. For Native American wisdom to be of use to people today, they need to understand the truth.

In order to grasp the significance of the different cultures and lifestyles of Native Americans it is important to look at the components of their civilisations that could become or have been of help to the formation of today's world, as well as the areas in which they lived. While this could be a daunting task, considering all the varieties of topographic and climatic regions in a land as vast as the Americas, I will simplify this by dealing with the United States within North America, breaking this down into four regions: the Eastern Woodlands, the Southwest Desert, the Northwest Coast and the Plains. In making these distinctions you need to understand that there will be some Natives who will not be covered, and that I must make some general statements that will not hold absolutely true for all the peoples in these regions. I do not have the space to cover every variation that exists, but only to help you on the way to a more accurate understanding of Native America.

EASTERN WOODLANDS

The inhabitants of this area were the first people met by the English, French and Dutch explorers as the age of invasion began in earnest, before the reign of Queen Elizabeth I. The majority of these first contacts with the aboriginals of North America proved to be very peaceful. There are many accounts by fishing boat captains as well as explorers that give evidence of this. In most cases aid as well as goods were given to the Europeans. In fact, one ship's captain was made very wealthy through his acquisition of sassafras from native farmers. (Sassafras is a tree that is used medicinally, at the time, it was purported to be a wonder cure for many ailments, including syphilis.)

Even after the beginnings of colonisation, the Native Americans were responsible for the success of the colonies. The story of Pocahontas saving Roanoke Colony leader John Smith from execution is factual in its foundation, even though it has become highly romanticised. The ensuing friendship did indeed contribute to the success of the struggling colony. Further to that account, it was the Powhattan people that came to the rescue of the colony of Jamestown when, without the aid given by the local natives, the English colonists reverted to cannibalism. The people of the Eastern Woodlands

have given so much to the modern world that is seldom
recognised.

The many Algonquian Nations, the Iroquois confederacy, and the 'five civilised tribes' (Choctaw, Chickisaw,
Cherokee, Seminole and Cree), made up the majority of
the population of the Eastern Woodlands. Their lifestyle
was primarily agricultural and they lived in stationary
towns that were surrounded by their cultivated fields.
Their crops consisted primarily of what was known by
the natives as 'the three sisters': corn (maize), beans and
squash.

Agriculture was not their only means of livelihood.
Among them were great hunters, craftsmen and traders,
and there existed, long before the advent of the colonial-
ists, an extensive trade system that extended up and down
the east coast of North America and beyond.

The area in which these people lived was extensively
wooded; forests that began on the coast stretched west-
ward over the mountains into the heartland of the continent. The native inhabitants of this vast forest lived
mostly along the rivers and tributaries, making use of the
waterways as a source of food, through fishing, as well as
using them for travel, usually in craft made of dugout logs
or birchbark canoes. They often travelled hundreds of
miles from their villages to trade in goods and materials
not available in their home areas.

Within the villages there was a highly structured
organisation, in many cases a democratic political system
that is to this day unequalled. Rumours of the freedom

and individual liberty that abounded among the Natives of the Americas was first evidenced in the publication in 1516 of *Utopia* by Sir Thomas More. The ideas that evolved through his writings came from the accounts of many explorers, which, upon their return to Europe, were published and read by the educated across the continent. One of the most influential accounts came from Amerigo Vespucci, the cartographer in whose honour America was named.

In the Eastern Woodlands, in the area that is now identified as upstate New York, was the seat of the Iroquois confederacy, to whom the peoples of the world should look when seeking to learn the source of democracy. Prior to 1450 there were five independent Nations: the Mohawk, Onondaga, Seneca, Cayuga and Oneida. Through the efforts of Hiawatha and Deganwidah, these five Nations formed the world's first constitutional democracy.

Within this democracy, governing bodies in each of the five Nations were elected by the citizens of the respective Nation. These elected officials (*sachems*) dealt with the laws that pertained to their Nation and chose or elected the representatives who would attend the council of the confederacy; the confederacy council dealt with the laws and business that concerned all the Nations of the confederacy collectively. This is the basic format of democratic government in today's world. The United States took this form directly from the Iroquois, then the French and British followed suit with their individual adaptations.

However, none of those that copied the Iroquois went as far as they did in ensuring equality and democratic safeguards. An example of this is the fact that within the Iroquois confederacy women had an equal vote to the men by 1450. In addition, if the women of one of the Nations determined that the representative was not acting in the best interest of his electorate, they had the power to recall and replace him.

Compare this to the way in which women were, and sometimes still are, looked upon in the 'civilised' world, it would seem there is a long way to go before the modern world catches up with the Iroquois of the 1450s.

SOUTHWEST DESERT

The peoples of the Southwest Desert are vastly different from the Eastern peoples. Their homes, lifestyles and political structures appear, to the outsider, to be alien to the other Natives of North America.

The difference in topography is drastic as well. Here is a land that looks to most to be barren, desolate and inhospitable. This is the land of the Painted Desert, Monument Valley, Death Valley and the Grand Canyon. The first Europeans to enter this land were the Conquistadors of Spain, in search of the fabled cities of gold. In the process they believed several times that they had found them. As they searched they came across a number of towns/ villages that in the golden light of a sunrise or sunset, from a distance, appeared to be made of gold; the reality was very disappointing.

In this semi-arid region are a number of peoples identified as Pueblo. This is a Spanish term that merely identifies the fact that they lived in towns that upon close examination were a lot like those found in Spain at that time. The dwellings that these people lived in were also reminiscent of Spain, with houses made of stone and sun-dried brick. In addition, it was found that, as in Spain, the livelihood of these peoples was agricultural.

The Pueblos of the Hopi, Zuni, Pima and others had fields of corn, beans and squash around them. In the tradition of most, if not all of these peoples, only the women were owners of the homes, fields and the crops that came from the fields. Women held the power within the family. This is a tradition that has survived even to this day; I found evidence of this when I visited the Hopi in 1994.

At the time of my visit I was involved in an attempt to help the Hopi with a problem they were having with their water supply. The problem stemmed from the misuse of precious fresh water by the largest opencast mining operation in North America. As a result of my involvement I was asked to attend a meeting between the Hopi and the mining company.

On the last week of my stay with the Hopi I learned from Alice, the secretary of President Sekakuku (then president of the Hopi Tribe Government), that she was to spend all of Friday night preparing a feast to be presented to the family of a young man that her youngest sister was interested in.

In the tradition of the Hopi, if a couple are interested in each other then the women of the girl's family will present a feast to the women of the man's family. What happens next will determine whether the couple are allowed to see each other or not. If the feast is refused then permission is denied and the young lady and young man will have to look to others for a partnership. Should the feast be accepted, however, then the couple will date and eventually marry.

When this marriage takes place, the women of the bride's family will provide a home for the couple and the groom will leave his mother's house and move in with his bride. Hereafter he will work the fields of his wife's family and only seldom return to the village of his mother. If the marriage should end in divorce, however, the man returns to the home of his mother.

Another parallel between the peoples of the Pueblos and the Spanish was their attention to religious matters. There is, in each village, at least one Kiva, a structure that is built partly underground with its only entrance being by means of a ladder through a hole in the roof of the structure. It is here that the spiritual matters of the community are taken care of. The Kiva, like the church, was the centre of the community's activities, and throughout the year different ceremonies and celebrations took place.

You must not, however, be mislead into thinking that

there is a great deal of similarity between the actions of the people that follow the way of the Kiva and those perpetuated by the churches of Europeans. The similarities are only superficial as will become evident as you learn more.

Other peoples found in the Southwestern Desert are the Apache, Comanche, Kiowa and Navajo, all very different to the Pueblos.

The Navajo I will spend no time discussing, except to make it clear that they are newcomers to this land. The Navajo invaded this area after the first Conquistadors and were able to adapt well by means of adopting many of the ways of those already there.

The other peoples were semi-nomadic, a lifestyle I will be discussing in greater detail in the section 'High Plains'.

NORTHWEST COAST

Here are a people that live on the edge of the sea and on the many islands that lie along the coast, cut off from the rest of the continent by the Rocky Mountains. The land we are now to look at runs from the far northwest of Washington State through the western province of Columbia, Canada, and well into Alaska.

It was a mere 35 years before the revolution/rebellion that gave birth to the United States, that these people were 'discovered'. The first contact with them was not made by Western European nations but by the Russians.

When the first ships sailed into the ancient harbours and began trading with the peoples of these towns, that had been in the same locations for thousands of years, they were warmly welcomed.

At this time in history the Russians and Europeans were seeking furs, and the Natives, having been in this land for so many millennia, had well-established trade connections with each other. Acquisition of furs and transport through their trade routes was an active part of their civilisations. When the Europeans tried to dominate and take over the long-established trade industry, conflict began.

The Nations of Natives that I speak of are the Eyak, Tlinglit, Haida, Kwakiutl, Salish, Makah and Chinook, to name but a few. Their villages were made up of a number of houses as well as communal buildings, and were almost always located on a coastal harbour. Transport was primarily by water, either sea or river.

Their homes were made of logs and planks hewn from trees; the land boasted an abundance of cedar, spruce and hemlock in forests that crowded right up to the narrow beaches along the shores. Each house would be large enough to accommodate up to 50 members of an extended family in comfort. Boats were of importance for trade as well as fishing and hunting the mammals of the sea, and were hewn from the largest of the trees, usually red cedar. All the peoples of this region were skilled boat makers, but the Haida were the most renowned. Their boats, up to 60 feet in length, with two masts with sails (for long sea journeys), and capable of transporting up to eight tons of cargo, were much valued for trade.

The work of women and men was clearly defined in these civilisations. The men hunted and trapped the animals of the land, fished the mammals of the sea, worked the wood of the forest to build their homes and boats and carved the planks and totem poles that they are renowned for. The women were occupied with gathering plant foods, maintaining the family homes and weaving the famous Chilkat and ravenstail robes.

Family and society were formed around a clan system. Ancestry is traced through the mother, so theirs was a matrilineal culture, thus the woman was held in great esteem. The raising and teaching of children was done by the mother's family. Boys were taught what they needed by their maternal uncles; girls were raised by their mother and her sisters. Even properties and land were passed on in this way. A person wouldn't inherit from their father but from their maternal uncles. Social structure was based on the clan that a person was born into, and then, for the men, that they married into.

The art of these people is world famous today. Few are not familiar with the herringbone design of the ravenstail robe that went into mass production during the Victorian age. The most recognised image that comes from this region, however, is the totem pole.

The people of the Northwest were the originators of the totem pole, and still use them in a traditional way. The images depicted on the poles, contrary to historical perception, are not gods. This interpretation is based on the egocentricity of the European cultures that have a philosophy of always being right and therefore superior. It is this attitude that led the 'civilised' world to its present day lack of understanding of the past, as well as things that appear different. It is also this that has led to a search for knowledge and wisdom by so many individuals.

The totem pole, along with most other carvings from this region, contains imagery of the creatures of nature that these people shared their lives with. The clans and societies were named after animals; the stories that were passed down through generations tell of the relationship between the carved characters and their human counterparts. This relationship with the natural world runs through all aspects of their societal, cultural, family and individual lives.

A final point regarding the peoples of the Northwest, that makes them unique among the Natives of North America, is the fact that they have never been placed on reservations. In the course of history the advancement of the dominant European-based civilisation not only conquered the Native Nations but in many cases re-located them from their ancestral homeland. This was not the case on the Northwest coast.

Here, the impact of the incoming Europeans was just as great as in other areas in respect of bringing vast changes to their lives, but it has not forced them from their ances-tral homes. Native towns still exist and can be located on modern maps. However, they do tend to be far different today from the way they were when the people of European descent began to move into them. The cities of Juneau and Sitka are large, modern Tlinglit villages, while towns like Ketchican, Wrangell, Kake and Angoon are expanded from their original Native forms. All of these places and more were the home villages of the Natives I have been talking about, and are still home to many of the original peoples of this land.

HIGH PLAINS

The most commonly known Natives – the nomadic hunters and gatherers depicted by Hollywood – are the peoples known as the Cheyenne, Arapaho, Blackfoot, Crow, Pawnee and Sioux, to name just a few.

The peoples of the plains were those identified as tipi dwelling, horseback hunters of buffalo, and warriors. Among them were such famous men of history as Black Kettle, Roman Nose, Satank, Sitting Bull and Red Cloud, identified by most of the inhabitants of modern Western civilisation as 'American Indians'. This came about not because these people were any greater than the others or because of their great numbers. In fact the peoples of the plains were a minority in relation to those that lived a more static lifestyle.

It was this image of a free life, presented by their nomadic existence, and their dress that has been the cause of so much romanticism. This coupled with the fact that they were the last to be defeated in the 'Indian Wars', has kept their image alive and inspired the imagination of people throughout the world. The true life of the plains Indian was far from the idyllic dreams of people today, however.

The temperature in summer can reach 110 degrees in the shade, in this land where trees are few and far between. Then winter sets in and the temperature is known to drop to 30 degrees below zero. During these times there is still the need to hunt and gather enough meat and other foods to feed everyone, collect the material for fires for warmth and cooking, maintain a reasonable supply of clothing, as well as provide and maintain all the other necessities of life for all the people of each village. Not as easy a life as people of today imagine, but at the same time not a bad life for those who knew well how to live in close harmony with their surroundings.

Theirs was, again, a unique society; this time a patriarchal society where the male was the head of the family and lineage traced through the father. The Europeans who first encountered these people perceived similarities between their own type of male dominance and that among the Natives they encountered. Those similarities were only superficial, however, and as usual, vastly misinterpreted. The Natives did indeed have a patriarchal system that didn't show the women in the forefront of dealings with the strange newcomers to their lands, but the position of the women was far more egalitarian than that of the invading 'civilisation'.

Women owned the tipi, the food supplies, in fact everything other than the men's personal clothing, tools, weapons and horses. It was the men's duty to hunt, fish, care for the horses, protect the community and deal with matters of council and law. It was the women's place to make the best use of what was provided so their family could live well, and to perform the day-to-day tasks of village life. Neither had an easy task and while, to outsiders, the women appeared to do most of the hard labour, the work of each sex was different but equally difficult.

The structure of the culture was one of clans and societies. Each group, be it a society of women or hunters, had a different role to play in the organisation of each village's life. At different times their roles would put the various members in the forefront of leadership. For example, in the Spring, when the food supplies would have been depleted through the hard winter, a hunting society would take the lead and organise the village to move to a place where hunting would be successful and where the women would have the opportunity to gather fresh plant foods and restock on fire material. At other times, when the physical needs of the people were fulfilled, leadership of the village would be taken over by a medicine society to arrange for gatherings and festivals that were more to do with the spiritual needs of the village. Then, in times of danger, a war society would take the role of leadership.

Individuals within each village would have the freedom to choose the part they would play in each event throughout their lives, but the leaders elected by a society or village were chosen for their success and skill in the realm of what was needed to be accomplished. A master (or expert) at hunting would be selected to lead the hunt, a successful fighter would be chosen to lead in war, and a person who was strong in Spirit would become the Holy Person. I have been very careful in the use of my terms here because all of these positions could be filled by women as well as men. In the culture of the plains Indian an individual had much more freedom to cross the sex boundaries than we have, even in this modern 'enlightened' time.

It was this individual freedom of both men and women

that probably caused many of the misunderstandings about us. For example, there were times when our leaders and wise people were not allowed to speak for us because of the invaders' concept that women were not worthy of their attention. It is for this reason that so many great women of our Nations, as well as the European-founded Nations, are not mentioned in the history books.

TODAY'S NATIVE AMERICAN

In the eyes of many people throughout the world, the Native American became suspended in time during the 19th century. Surprisingly, this belief exists even in the modern Nations that surround us in North America. Many Canadians and New Americans think that the original Natives have all disappeared. In Europe it is even worse.

Let me re-emphasise the fact that we are still in existence. In today's world you can meet an original Native American in almost any location on earth and seldom be able to differentiate them from other peoples. We come in all shapes, sizes and appearances. We no longer dress in our ancestral clothing except for important events. Some of us are highly educated, in the academic sense, and hold a wide variety of jobs, including doctors, lawyers, accountants, even politicians.

Contrary to popular belief, therefore, we too have become modern ... to a degree. There were, however, a couple of common threads that ran through my accounts of the four geographical areas that I feel make us remain somewhat unique in today's world. One that is important, though I won't dwell on it, is the difference in the position of the women in our cultures. The second is the more relevant, and may be the reason why our women were able to be in that position. It is our universal attachment to and respect for the earth and the natural world that we are all a part of. This universal connection is, in my opinion, what prevents us from becoming totally lost to the ways of modern 'civilised' life.

Through the latter half of the 20th century the unification of many different Native American peoples has been evidenced in a variety of ways. This relatively new trend of cross-cultural unity between so many varying cultures is one that has come about for a variety of reasons, not least of which is the ever shrinking world syndrome; the ease of long distance communication and travel have brought many previously isolated peoples closer together.

Another aspect that has brought us closer together, in a potentially negative way, is a survival element. There is a need to be commercial in order to live in the modern world, and this need has caused people to do some strange things. One such example took place on the Alabama-Coshota reservation in Texas.

The reservation is located in a region that is economically depressed. During the 1970s subsistence farming and forestry were its two major industries and they were on the decline. The up and coming industry was tourism. This was helped by the proximity of the reservation to Houston, a large populated area less than a day's drive away. The people of the reservation therefore decided to capitalise on this, as well as on the rise in interest in Native Americans that was taking place.

The Alabama-Coshota built a 'traditional' village. It contained dwellings, meeting houses and craft displays, as well as dance, dress and music exhibitions. All these things were kept as close to tradition as possible. The tourists came. Then the tourists left, grumbling and vowing not to return. Some of the comments were along the lines of, 'How dare they copy white men's housing and clothing and pass it off as Indian?' Yet the Alabama-Coshota had *traditionally* lived in log-built long houses that resembled what most called log cabins and thought of as settlers' homes. They were also farmers who grew cotton and wove it into cloth long before the Europeans came to North America.

The next year, and still today as far as I know, tipis were erected on the reservation and the workers wore buckskin clothes and feathered bonnets. The tourists came back. There are many such instances where, in order to survive, Native Americans adapted their appearance to fit the imagination of others.

A stronger, and possibly a more powerful, way in which we have united is through adversity. It is recorded in the history books that the 'Indian Wars' ended at the 'battle' of Wounded Knee Creek in 1890. Yet it was not an end to the conflict between the Natives of North America and the New Americans, it was simply the time when the method of battle began to change.

Slowly and with great difficulty, we began to understand the ways of the new order of things as they were forced upon us. From the 1890s, the peoples of the plains (the last to be defeated) joined the others in the transition that had begun at the dawn of the European colonisation of our lands. In many ways we were aided by well intentioned, though misguided, peoples, in learning the new ways. Our children were removed from their families and taught the language and mechanics of the dominant society.

Through the few generations that followed the 'last battle', Native Americans have become as proficient at doing battle in classrooms and courtrooms as our ancestors were in violent conflict. Throughout the 1960s we learnt about non-violent protest by observing the descendants of slaves gain more power, and in the early 1970s we began to regain some of our old strengths using new methods and new alliances.

Many of our Nations were represented in the occupation of the Bureau of Indian Affairs in Washington DC, many were involved in the occupation of Alcatraz in San Francisco, and there were many that gave physical and moral support to those at the second battle of Wounded Knee in 1973, when a small band of Native Americans held the FBI, US Marshal Service and Bureau of Indian Affairs police at bay for several days in order to draw the world's attention to the plight of the Native American people. These are just a few examples of the 'new' battles that we have fought against the New Americans in the United States. There are many more that have been waged in courtrooms, where advances in regaining our lives and retaining our heritage have occurred.

The United States is not the only place in which this conflict is still occurring though. As recently as 1990, Native Americans united in support of a group of Natives that were defending sacred ground from development in Canada. A small group of Natives were set upon by Canadian troops when they objected to a golf course being built on a burial site.

I could give many such accounts of the evolution of Native America into the modern world's realm, but the most important is the common ground that has allowed us to grow strong again as individuals. It is that common ground, the belief and wisdom of our ancestors, that is most important. The things that we have found to unite us and make ourselves and our cultures strong can also help peoples of other backgrounds to develop their own strengths and connections. In the following chapters I will attempt to supply the reader with the tools that have aided us, to help them on their own life path.

2

THE MEDICINE WHEEL

In the early years of my life I was treated in much the same way as the children of my people were treated before formal education was introduced. Then, a child was allowed to explore its world and to seek knowledge and understanding by experience and questioning. Very little restraint was imposed upon a child in their quest to experience and learn of life. There was virtually nothing that anyone would stop the child from learning about.

This attitude, held by my grandparents, allowed me to be privy to many conversations and activities that the adults of my household were involved in. I was also allowed to question and receive explanations that many children are denied, even in today's 'enlightened' society.

It was through the opportunity of being able to listen in on adult conversations that I first became aware of the term 'Medicine Wheel'. This led me to question my grandfather about its meaning.

Due to my young age, his explanation was, at first, very simplistic. We were sitting on the front porch of our house and he went out into the yard and gathered a handful of stones. Then, sitting down on the plank floor beside me, he laid the stones out in the shape of the Wheel. This was the beginning of my search for an understanding of the Medicine Wheel.

This hoop is many things and is understood in many ways. It is the circle of life in all its forms and manifestations; it is a tool for teaching; it is an instrument of understanding; it manifests itself into a way of thinking; it is life itself.

In order for you to begin to understand the term itself you must first examine the meanings of the words. When dealing with the English language terms can be easily misunderstood because not everyone understands the words in the same way. So let's break it down.

The word 'wheel' is not too confusing; everyone has a common understanding of what a wheel is or represents. In order to fully grasp the concept as it is intended here, you need only to understand that the terms 'circle', 'hoop' and 'cycle' could all be used in place of 'wheel'.

The word medicine is the more confusing of the two words. In the modern or Western civilised world the term 'medicine' has a different meaning to that understood by Native Americans. The Oxford Dictionary defines medicine as: *1. the science or practice of the diagnosis, treatment, and prevention of disease; 2. a compound or preparation used for the treatment or prevention of disease.* In both these definitions there is an understanding that something is wrong and medicine is the means of correction. The Native American use of the term 'medicine' could be better defined as communication; communication on all levels and by all means.

When medicine is considered in this way, humans practise medicine whenever they meet for whatever purpose. Medicine is taking place in every conversation, at every talk or lecture; in fact, medicine takes place even when there are no words being spoken. Consider the communication that occurs through body language: facial expressions, eye contact (or lack of), even hand signals (both aggressive and friendly). It's all this and more that is meant by the term 'medicine', and it is here that an understanding of the Medicine Wheel can begin.

In infancy the first medicine that occurs does so through our senses in a very rudimentary fashion. We take years to develop coherent language and initially rely upon symbolic communication. The symbols begin in a crude fashion and as we grow and develop they become more intricate. The same is true of the Medicine Wheel.

To begin, the Wheel is a visual, physical symbol like the circles of stone that began my own journey of understanding. Where is the beginning of a circle? Where is its end? The concept that it doesn't have either causes a great deal of confusion to the educated peoples of the West. In order to alleviate this, let us first examine some ways in which the Medicine Wheel can be used.

CYCLES OF LIFE

There are three main cycles of our existence: the day, the year and the whole of a lifetime. Everything we do falls within each and every one of these cycles, and each of these has a beginning and an end.

Looking at them separately it is easy to recognise the Western way of seeing things in straight lines. When you look at an appointment diary the times of a day are laid out in a line from the day's beginning to its end. And when you look at a year planner there are, again, straight lines from the beginning to the end of the year. In history books you find timelines drawn out to show the beginning of a lifetime or period of history, followed by the events that took place until the end of the life or period. Learning and dealing with things only in this way causes us to think in straight lines.

The Medicine Wheel enables us to think in circles. This can lead to confusion, so to start I will go through it in much the same way as I began to learn about this circle of life as a five-year-old. Our first task is to establish a place of beginning.

The Beginning

In the cycle of a day we are taught that the beginning is the moment past midnight. Yet for a people of the natural world, without timepieces to show when that moment is, or even the ability to see well in the darkness that would surround a person during that part of the cycle of a day, there would be no concept of beginning at that time. The time for the beginning of a day would have to occur at the time when all the senses could recognise it: the dawn. As we are a creature of the light, our day truly starts when the sun rises and we are able to see it.

The East of the Wheel

With the beginning of a day being at sunrise, the starting point on the Medicine Wheel is the east. This is the direction of the sunrise. The power of the light gives us the sense of a new beginning, coming out of the darkness of the night, gradually giving us a clear vision as the sun rises above the horizon and fills our day with its power.

To follow the same line of thought, a problem also arises if you consider the beginning of a year to be on January 1. Looking at the natural world you will find that this is close to the darkest time of the year. It is the equivalent of the night-time of a year. Every thing is sleeping, at rest, waiting for the light.

The beginning of the year is the Spring. This is when the natural world begins to waken. The trees sprout buds, then open their leaves and grow anew, reaching for the light as the days grow longer. The seeds that fell to the ground in the previous year and the seeds planted by those that till the soil begin to sprout up out of the dark earth, reaching for the light of the sun. Birds and other creatures undertake the process of mating and birthing. This is the time of beginning, this is the east of the year.

The same position holds true as the beginning place on the Wheel of a lifetime. We all start our lives in the east. This is the time of the infant, or new-born.

In today's world of advanced technology there is a great deal of dispute over when a life begins. Some say it is at the time of conception; others say it is at a certain time of foetal development. If we seek a more simple understanding, it could be reasonable to consider that a child's life begins when it is separated from the mother's body and begins its life as an individual human being. This is the time of birth, when the infant leaves the darkness within the womb and comes out into the light to start its journey towards a path of independent life.

The Power of the East   In examining anything to do with the Medicine Wheel, it is necessary to remember that this is the circle of life. As such it contains a life-force, and energy, or as I learned, a power. Given the complexity of life, it is said that each part of life has a power of its own. Thus, each direction of the Wheel has its own power.

You should already be aware that a power of the east is light; the light of the natural world that is evident at the rising of the sun, the sunlight that the plants reach for in the Spring, and the light that allows us to see and grow after our birth.

There is more to this power than the physical power of sunlight, however, just as there is more to us humans than the physical aspect of our existence. As a child I became fully aware of this in a strange way.

Like most children, I was addicted to television. One Saturday morning I was watching a cartoon in which a man was at work at a bench. You could tell that he was having difficulty in figuring out the project that he was working on because there was a question mark over his head. Suddenly, that question mark changed. He finally figured out the solution to his dilemma, and I knew this because the question mark had changed into a light bulb.

This was an exciting event for me because I too achieved a solution to a dilemma at that moment. I had spent days, weeks, months, trying to fathom some of the lessons that my grandfather had given me about the powers of the Medicine Wheel. Then, suddenly, I understood; the power of the east is not just the power of physical light but also the power of enlightenment.

Enlightenment or understanding is something that evolves slowly throughout the life of a human. We are constantly learning and achieving this over the course of our lives. It has often been said that we 'learn something new every day'. Being aware of this is to be constantly seeking to face the east in search of the light of understanding.

Finally, the power of an infant is the power of dependency. Though now a separate being, an infant has no ability to provide for itself. Yet it has a power to communicate its needs and compel others to provide for it. Many look upon this dependency as a weakness, yet it is something that we all deal with within ourselves throughout our lives.

The Natural Way

In the native, or primitive, way of things it is always the natural way that is our guide. It is for this reason that the journey around the Wheel goes in a sunwise, or clockwise, direction. Have you ever considered why the hands on all clocks and watches travel in the same direction? Wouldn't it be more interesting if, for instance, they made watches with hands that travelled anti-clockwise for left-handed people? The reason why this didn't happen was because the first maker of a mechanical timepiece was mimicking the natural world. He took his lesson from the natural evidence he found around him.

Take a stick and set it into the ground in an open place on a sunny day. Then watch the way the shadow of the stick travels around it as the day progresses: sunwise.

The Time of the Child

Just as with everything that lives, the Wheel is in a state of constant change. The sun travels throughout the day from sunrise to the noon of the day. Spring slowly develops into Summer. The infant grows into the child. This is the time of the south, the second quarter of the Medicine Wheel.

The South of the Wheel

In the course of a day the most active time is midday. This is when the majority of people are at their peak. Even those that felt tired as a result of the night before are now fully awake and active. For signs of this peak of activity, stand opposite an office building around noon and watch the mass exodus as the workers escape for lunch; or sit through the morning on a high street and observe the increased flow of people around the noon hour. It's the same in nature; as the day warms, the activity in the natural world increases.

The same holds true in the Summer of the year. This is the time of the greatest amount of growth in the natural world, when the trees and plants are involved most in the act of what scientists call photosynthesis – converting the sun's energy into growth on their journey toward maturity.

This too is the most active time of a human's lifetime. Those of you who have ever dealt with growing children will recognise this. Consider the amount of time and energy an adult consumes in an attempt to keep up with a toddler.

The Power of the South   All adults have within them an awareness of the power of the south. This is the power of a child, and even those without children have memories of their own childhood. Some memories are pleasant and some are not, but all are evidence of a child's power. There are times when this power is looked upon as weakness rather than strength, but it is still a significant part of every human.

In order to examine and understand this power you need only to observe the activities of a toddler. This is the beginning of the time of the child. No longer an infant that must rely upon another to provide for every need, now a development and sense of independence begins to evolve. The ability to use utensils and eat rather than be fed, no longer having to be carried because they can first crawl, then walk. Exploration, examination and adventure has become the order of the day.

For the child, everything seems to happen at high speed. They never seem to do anything at a leisurely pace, moving from one thing to another at such a rate that it seems that it would sap the energy of three adults just to keep up. The child is always questioning, as well. The development of speech rapidly leads to the questions: why?, how?, when?, what?, and are we there yet?, all of which form a major part of the vocabulary of the child. For a while, at least, they believe the answers that are given by any adult.

The power of a child is therefore curiosity, innocence and trust. To observe this, just give a toddler a new toy. The first thing they do is put it in their mouth (to see what it tastes like). Then shove it in an ear (to hear it better). Next they take it apart to see how it works (until it doesn't). Finally it is given back to you with the sure knowledge that you will be able to fix it.

No matter how old, experienced or cynical we get, everyone retains, in varying degrees, the power of the child. It is always necessary to have curiosity or we would stagnate and fail to learn new things. There are also times when we must trust others because no one can live their lives in total, independent isolation. And we all have a sense of innocence about us. This innocence is probably the hardest to admit to, yet every day we hear about terrible things that happen to other people, such as accidents, fires and robberies, and we innocently believe that those things only happen to others.

As adults there are powers of the child within us that

we should nurture and enjoy. As an adult, we can still enjoy playing, excitement, innocence, curiosity and so forth. There are also some aspects of these powers that need to be recognised and dealt with in a cautious manner in order to develop balance and well-being.

The Look Within Time

Now we reach the time of the adult. This is the culmination of the growth period of a human, when we should recognise the aspects of the infant and child that we were, and develop a sense of our maturity so that we can make the best use of our gifts. In the way I learned of the Medicine Wheel, this is the time when the individual must look to themselves for an understanding of how to proceed in life.

The West of the Wheel

Having passed from sunrise, through the full course of the light of day, we have arrived at the time of darkness. The west is the time of the setting sun, when it begins to become difficult to see.

In the course of a year it is the time when the nights begin to draw in and the wind blows colder. The plants that sprang from the earth in Spring are now at the peak of their growth and are ready to be harvested. The trees now put on their brightest colours before losing their leaves to the winter winds. It is Autumn.

In a human lifetime the individual has stepped into the adult phase of their life. This is the time that the child looked forward to, thinking that the adult time of their life would be a time of freedom and satisfaction, when they would know the answers to all problems, and when they would be complete in their knowledge about all the troublesome things in life.

Then we reach the time of our adulthood to discover that our lives and the questions that life brings have only just begun. It is the dark time – if we allow it to be.

In my own search, the writings of Carl Jung helped me explain this time of the adult the best. To paraphrase the lesson as I understand it:

We begin life and travel through to its end with only one thing that never leaves us: our shadow. This shadow is like a dark sack that we carry over our shoulder everywhere we go. As we go through our lives we find out things about ourselves that we don't want others to know about and we hide them in the sack. Then we look at ourselves and see things that we don't want to admit to and we hide them in the sack.

This goes on until we are an adult and the sack is too heavy to bear. Then we start to unearth the things that we hid and deal with them.

The Power of the West   The power of the west is a difficult issue to discuss because of the complexity of the life of an adult. Therefore it is necessary to simplify things. In my or our tradition, the way that I was able to develop my understandings was through a story that demonstrates the powers of the west.

This is a story of past times, when all the different peoples of the world gave freely to others and all peoples could understand each other. In these times the four-legged peoples gave of themselves to help other four-legged as well as the two-legged. The winged ones did all they could to help those bound to the land and everyone could communicate freely with all peoples.

Everyone had gifts that were unique and all were willing to share their gifts.

In those days there were several creatures that are not seen in today's world, and little is known of them, although they still exist.

One of these was a Red Hawk. This Hawk was the most beautiful bird that anyone had ever seen. The sound that it made would cause all that heard it to stop and listen. This beauty of vision and sound was the gift that the Red Hawk had to share. It would travel around the world each year, visiting all and displaying its beauty of sight and sound in exchange for the things it needed to live.

Other peoples were the Thunderbeings. These people lived far to the west, high in the mountains. Their gift was the gift of keeping the gate that holds the clouds back. When the peoples and the earth needed rain the Thunderbeings opened the gate and allowed the clouds to cross the sky and the rains to fall. Then when enough rain had fallen they would call the clouds back and close the gate. Due to the nature of their gift the Thunderbeings never travelled from the mountains and few people ever visited them due to the arduous trek to reach them.

The Red Hawk would visit them, though, and display his beauty of vision and sound. Yet these Thunderbeings were not as appreciative of his gifts as others were. In fact they did little but complain, no matter what he did. If he stood in the sun they would shield their eyes and complain that the brightness hurt them. If he stood in the shade they would squint and complain that he was difficult to see. When the Hawk sang they said it was either too loud or too soft. The Thunderbeings were never satisfied. Finally the Red Hawk grew tired of the Thunderbeings' complaints and stopped visiting them. This left them complaining to each other about not having any visitors.

After some time had passed the Thunderbeings decided to do something about their lack of visitors. One year they refused to open the gates. With no rain the grass dried up leaving the grass eaters hungry. After a time the streams stopped flowing and the lakes dried up. There was much suffering and death throughout the world. The peoples began to cry out for help and the Great Spirit heard their cries.

However, the Great Spirit does not often directly intercede in the affairs of the earth. Rather than open the gates and allow the rains to come, Great Spirit called the Red Hawk to it and gave the Hawk additional gifts of a very special dance and a very special song. Once the Hawk had received its instruction it went to the top of a hill and called the peoples to help. The Hawk told them to gather material and build a lodge. When this was accomplished the Hawk went into the lodge and shut the door.

Soon the dance began. As the feet of the Hawk struck the ground the earth trembled and shook. The trembling and shaking of the ground beneath the feet of the Thunderbeings made them afraid.

Then the song began and the sound of it was heard all over the earth. The sound of the song had a power in it that compelled the Thunderbeings to open the gates. The clouds rushed across the sky and the rains fell. The grass grew green. The streams began to flow and the lakes grew full.

Then the Hawk stopped his singing and dancing. The rains stopped. The clouds drew back and the gates were closed. When the Red Hawk stepped out of the lodge the sun reflected off its back and the sky was filled with rainbows. People from all around praised the Hawk and thanked it for the help received from its gifts.

The event of building the lodge, dancing the dance and singing the song became an annual event. As the years passed the Hawk grew very proud of the gifts and luxuriated in the praise received as a result of them.

Then one year the people gathered to build the lodge and the Red Hawk stopped them, saying: 'How can anyone truly appreciate the beauty and intricacy of the steps in my dance? The walls of the lodge have always concealed them from sight. How can the people hear the true magnificence of the song when it is always muffled by the walls of the lodge?'

So, that year, no lodge was built.

Everyone present stood in awe of the beauty of the song and the intricacy of the dance. The gates opened, the clouds crossed the sky and the rains came. Then when it had rained enough the Red Hawk stopped. But *the rains didn't!*

Rivers broke their banks, lakes flooded the plains, and many people suffered and died in the floods. Those on the highest ground cried out for help and Great Spirit looked down to see what had happened.

This time Great Spirit took direct action. The rains were stopped, the clouds pushed back and the gates closed. No rainbows filled the sky this year. On the top of the hill, head hung in shame, stood the Red Hawk.

Great Spirit again called the Red Hawk to it and that is the last time anyone living on earth has been able to see it.

Now the Red Hawk lives in service to the Thunderbeings, no longer compelling them to perform their gift but serving them in punishment for misuse of his own gifts. Now the Hawk is never seen by the descendants of the people that loved it so. Now the sound it makes strikes fear in those that hear it. Never can it look upon this world it loved without destroying what it sees. For the Red Hawk is now the Thunderbird. When it flaps its wings to push the clouds across the sky the fearsome sound of thunder is heard. When there is a break in the clouds and it looks down, the light from its eye is the bolt of lightning that blinds us from being able to see it and destroys whatever it looks upon.

The powers of the west are the same as the powers of the Thunderbird: the powers of fear and destruction. Learning to deal with the fearful and destructive nature that is part of us all is similar to learning to deal with the thunderstorm.

To look into the darkness within is a frightening thing to do. The dark is where we have hidden the things that we see as being self-destructive, the things about ourselves that we are afraid to face. The darkness within is also a place that holds the unknown or those elements that cannot be understood, and these too are fearsome.

Consider how people react to the first sound of thunder. All will start with the fear of surprise as the first clap is heard before the storm. After that, reactions vary. Some will go out from their shelter and greet the coming storm with excitement. Then there are those that will just go to the door or window and watch the beauty of the storm from a safe place. There are also some who, like children, will remain in terror of the storm and hide under the bed.

We all fear the dark as we do the thunder. And the storm has lightning that is as potentially destructive as our own self-destructive nature. Yet the thing to remember about the storm is that what follows the thunder and lightning is the gift of rain. What is needed is to develop the ability to overcome the fear, avoid the self-destructive nature that lies within, and receive the gifts.

Everyone has been given all that they need to live their lives well. What the time of the west is about is identifying those gifts and making the best possible use of them.

The Final Quarter

Now we are nearing the end of the first part of our understanding of the Medicine Wheel. This is, in some respects, the most confusing to those who live and have been taught only in the ways of the modern world. This confusion is not too difficult to overcome if you will open your heart and mind to the old ways, the ways of understanding things that were common prior to industrialisation and modernisation, forces that have separated us from the natural rhythm of life.

The North of the Wheel

It is in this direction of the Wheel that the nights draw in as we approach the end of the year. Those that work with the land have harvested the crops from the fields and are busy preparing for the cold days and long nights of Winter. Activity doesn't stop, but it is altered and appears more sedentary.

In the course of a day, the sun has gone from the sky and the only natural light is that of the moon and the scattering of stars. Vision, in the physical way of seeing, is more difficult. We must now slow down and take time to rest from our physical labours.

So too is it in this stage of the human lifetime. It is time for physical activity to be slowed. Evidence of this comes to light if you reflect on some of the things we say when attempting to keep up with the more youthful. Things like, 'I'm not as young as I used to be', or 'I remember when ...'. These are symptomatic of the time of the north, when we begin to reflect on the past.

The Power of the North   When looking at the natural world you can see that slowing down of activities is indicative of the time of the north of the Wheel. All seems to slow almost to the point of looking as though it were dead. The sap falls from the trees and they lose their greenery. A great stillness pervades the land as the insect world disappears from view; even bird song is greatly altered as many species move from the northern areas to their winter habitats. The four-legged populations decrease as many species retire into their annual hibernation.

There is also a great alteration in human activity. Even in modern, industrial civilisation people are less prone to be outside the warm safety of buildings during the Winter. As the days grow shorter and the temperature begins to fall people tend to stay by the fire. For those who work close to nature, this too is the time of year to go indoors and begin the Winter chores.

Winter to the farmer is the time to take account of the

last year's activities. The tallies are done to calculate the yields that were harvested against the seed that was sown, plans are worked out for the planting time that will come in the Spring, and old equipment is renovated and repaired and the new tools that will make the next year's labours more productive are made.

This too was the way of the Winter for the Native Americans of history. Whether they were farmers or hunter-gatherers, the Winter was, primarily, the time to reflect on the past year's endeavours, to recount the stories of the past for the children to hear and learn from, and to make preparations for the Spring to come.

The time of the north is the same in a day, a year or a lifetime. It is a time of rest and reflection. It is a time of wisdom. So much of the circle of the Medicine Wheel is about learning, developing and growing. This is the time of understanding. There is much emphasis placed on learning in the modern world. Most of that learning comes down to the acquisition of information, which is important, but not as important as understanding. Understanding is wisdom.

Wisdom is much more elusive than knowledge. It is an arduous task to acquire and remember information, yet it is a task that all humans are capable of to greater and lesser degrees. The task of developing wisdom is a far greater chore, and at the same time seems to be easier for some.

Many would equate wisdom with old age. Among Native Americans there is a great deal of emphasis placed on the wisdom of the Elders. What is not clear to many is that Elder does not necessarily mean older. Many times I have heard people talk about the wisdom they see in children. There is an old adage that I learned sometime in the past that says, 'Out of the mouths of babes comes the wisdom of the ages'. Throughout my lifetime I have come across wise youths and foolish old people.

The time of the north is elusive, hidden in the darkness of the Winter and the night, yet it surfaces in people of any age.

PUTTING IT TO USE

Now that I have taken you all the way around the Wheel, in a way that is somewhat philosophical, I would like to offer you a method to help you begin to incorporate what you have read into personal use. Before we begin, I would suggest that you acquire a notebook in which to record your findings, thoughts and experiences so that you will be able to keep track of your development throughout your search for your own Medicine Wheel.

Quite a number of ceremonies could be offered that would enhance your awareness of the Medicine Wheel as a personal tool for life. However, a large number of these ceremonies require that you have a personal understanding of the workings of the Medicine Wheel within yourself. It is therefore best for everyone embarking on a search for understanding to start as a child and slowly develop, rather than begin too far along and lose their way.

EXERCISE

Constructing Your Own Medicine Wheel

♦ From wherever you can, acquire a collection of 13 stones. Then, in a place of safety, sit quietly and relax yourself.

♦ Examine your stones. Some of you will have chosen crystals or tumblestones that you purchased in shops, while others will have just picked stones at random, perhaps on a walk in a nearby park. Regardless of the source, look over each stone and choose by use of your feelings or intuition which four of them should represent the four directions of your wheel. As you make your choices remember what each direction represents.

♦ Now that you have chosen the four stones for each of the cardinal directions, set them out in their positions before you as though they were the points of a compass. Then place the remaining stones so that they form the shape of the drawing on page 24.

♦ At this point the way that you proceed is very much up to you. Prepare yourself in a way that makes you comfortable and at ease. Perhaps play some soft music or burn an incense stick or some oil in a burner. The aim is to set the atmosphere for you to enter what some call a meditation.

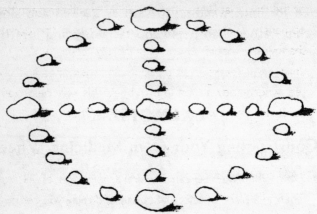

◆ Once you are prepared, relax into a position in front of the Medicine Wheel that you have constructed and concentrate on the stone that sits in the east. As you concentrate, reflect on the fact that this is a new beginning. Reflect on the times in your past that you have ventured on to new paths. Consider how these new beginnings evolved, as the Medicine Wheel of your life revolves, evolving from one beginning through the cycle of development, to the stage of maturity and on to the understandings and lessons that have been gained.

◆ Throughout the time of your meditation there will be events, experiences and lessons learned that will come to prominence. These are the ones to make note of. It is these memories that you should now examine in relation to the Wheel.

◆ Begin to consider where the events that you recall most clearly fit in with what you have begun to learn about the directions of the Wheel that is before you. Are the memories that come most clearly memories of the true child (in years) or the child that lives within the adult? Has there been development within you that you have hidden in the darkness/shadow self, that is now forcing its way to the surface to be dealt with? Record your thoughts and memories and try to see where they fit on the Wheel. This will help you to construct your own personal Medicine Wheel.

For many, the first experience of working with the Wheel in this way will continue to cause confusion. The reason for this is that it starts out seeming fruitless, without any clear conclusion. It is not neat and orderly because it is the beginning of thinking about things in a circle rather than a straight line. Persevere. As you read on and take part in some more advanced ceremonial exercises, things will develop more clearly for you.

3

WE ARE ALL RELATED

Within the order of things pertaining to the circle of life there is a belief that runs throughout the traditions of the Native Americans: that all of creation is interrelated.

In the native tongue of my ancestors there is a declaration that is rapidly becoming common to peoples of many backgrounds: 'MITAKUYE OYASIN'. Simply translated it means, 'We are all related'. It is not as simple a statement as it sounds, however. This is the statement that expresses the belief that led to Chief Seattle's speech; the speech that Chief Red Jacket made to the missionaries in 1805; and the tenets of the 'dreamers' as proclaimed by Smohalla in the 1850s–60s. The statement 'Mitakuye Oyasin' expresses a wholeness of life that is only grasped in fragments within the tradition of advanced Western civilisation. As with the straight line way of thinking versus the circular way of the Medicine Wheel, there are boundaries that must be broken down to fully grasp the concept of *'Mitakuye Oyasin'*.

I visit schools regularly, and when I ask the children what they think I mean when I say 'we are all related' the answer is quite often that we are related because we are all human. This is true, and a very important concept, although in many ways it is only a fragment of the whole concept. When a Native American says *'Mitakuye Oyasin'* they are referring to the interdependent relationship of all of creation.

THE PHYSICAL

In its most basic, primitive form, this interdependent relationship is easily recognised through observing the needs of survival that are fulfilled by other aspects of creation. The honour of this relationship is often lost, ignored or hidden in the complexity of life in the modern world. Living, as most of us do, in towns or villages, gathering our foods from shops and markets, it is easy to forget the source of our sustenance.

If we are to develop a more clear understanding of our place on the Medicine Wheel of creation, the first place to look is at the needs we have that are fulfilled by others. Mankind has spent many centuries at the top of the food chain. We gain our physical sustenance from a wider variety of food stuffs than any other creature on earth. Yet our arable farming and animal husbandry techniques are so alien to the natural way of things that they compound our separation from the natural world.

To a Native American following the old ways, the way of Western civilisation does not make sense. How can anything that lives be more or less important than any other thing? Everything that has come to be has a purpose and gift to give that will help others to live well. As humans we rely on a great number of plants and animals to fulfil our physical needs, yet less and less honour is given to the plants and creatures and more attention is paid to those people and institutions that present a finished product for the consumer. This separates us from the natural and falsely gives honour to an abusive, destructive, wasteful system.

In the old, or traditional ways, honour and respect was given to the hunter, farmer, and to those that produced items or products from the plants and animals. More importantly, honour, respect and attention was also given to the natural system and to those species that gave their life to aid and improve the life of the consumer. That honour, respect and attention is what is missing in today's world.

There are many that make an effort to alleviate the abuse, destruction and waste. However, they seem to be stuck in the tradition of straight line thinking. Their actions and ideas are still separated from the circle of the Medicine Wheel. Examples of these types of people include some vegetarians and animal rights activists.

There are many vegetarians that refuse to eat meat

because they 'can't stand the thought of an animal being killed'. This being their only consideration, they fail to look at the needs of their body and end up with ill health until they learn to balance and supplement their diet so all their needs are met. Also, in some instances, these same people that refuse to eat meat will find no relationship between that and the wearing of a good pair of leather shoes, a leather belt or coat. Somewhere the connection to the death of an animal and the wearing of its skin is lost.

In the case of animal rights activists, it is a commendable feeling, the desire to improve the life of animals. However, freeing species randomly into an area that has no natural defence against their predatory nature is an act of destruction and disrespect for the natural environment.

In no way am I saying that vegetarians are acting wrongly, or that the plight of animals being used in abusive husbandry practices should be ignored. The point of this lesson is to teach you to look at the entire circumstances of your actions. That way you will teach yourself to become aware and cause the least amount of harm to yourself and to the Medicine Wheel of life with your way of life.

The way of a traditional Native American is to look as closely as possible at the way in which their life benefits and affects *Mitakuye Oyasin*, 'all our relations'.

THE SPIRIT

When Native Americans are viewed by others they often see a connection that links us with the natural world. Most people have a mental image of a people clad in fringed buckskin and bedecked with feathers and furs. It is true that many of our ancestors dressed in this manner on a daily basis, but today this kind of attire is reserved for Pow-Wows and other special events. This is so for practical reasons. Today's physical lifestyle would make it impractical to dress in old traditional attire, but the reasons for the wearing of furs and feathers remain.

In past times, when our ancestors lived without the modern conveniences of cities, shops, manufactured clothing, and so on, they were required to deal directly with the hunting and gathering of the necessities of life. This put them in direct contact with the life and death of the others that fulfilled their needs. The balance and lessons of the natural world were part of their everyday life.

It was this close association with the other aspects of creation that developed an awareness of the Spirit that exists in other beings as well as in humans. Through the understanding that arose from recognising the Spirit, or soul, that all living things possess, there came a respect and honour towards each individual and a recognition that all things have a lesson for us to learn from them. These lessons are about how to live our lives in the physical, as well as giving guidance for our own Spirit.

The lives of the ancestors displayed their respect of the

other aspects of creation that had taught them lessons. Names such as Sitting Bull, Crazy Horse, Brave Eagle and Black Elk were carried by these people as a note of respect and honour to another that had given them guidance in Spirit. There were also clans and societies whose names reflected the source of the guiding Spirit: Bear Clans, Turtle Clans, Horse Societies, and so on. Today, a Spirit teacher is often referred to as a totem animal.

Totem guides are in evidence in many cultures, yet there seems to be little true understanding of them. The Bald Eagle of the United States, German Golden Eagle and British Lion are displays of totem animals. Each nation, state, family or individual that displays one of these totems is giving honour to the Spirit lessons that the life of that creature taught them. It is these lessons that people today must begin to relearn.

Lessons from the Natural World

Shields, whether they be Native American, family crests or heraldic, are all symbolic of the teachers of lessons. This is also true of most items known as 'artefacts'. There are many Native American artefacts available in shops throughout the world today.

One of the most readily available is the Dreamcatcher. Thousands of people buy them and read on the tags that they are used to keep people from having 'bad' dreams. This is a wonderful concept for a fairy tale, yet it has little foundation in the reality of a Dreamcatcher.

The Dreamcatcher, as I was taught, is a spider's web, and the lessons that we can learn from a spider are important to our lives. Many people don't like spiders, but that is usually a result of not knowing or respecting the lessons that can be learned from them.

The first lesson of the spider is bravery. When beginning to weave its web a spider will attach a thread that is so fine that it can hardly be seen by the naked eye to something and hurl itself off, swinging by that thread to reach another place to which to attach it. Consider the location of most spiders' webs. They tend to be in high, out of the way places. If we were to fall from that height we would, at the very least, break a bone. Yet the spider, who would also be injured from that fall, trusts the strength of that thread.

The next lesson that is taught by the spider is a lesson of beauty. Take a look at a spider's web; the web is always a thing of beauty, yet it is only a home, a trap, and a larder for the spider. The lesson here is that we should do or make whatever we need as beautiful as we can. I am not aware of a word meaning 'art' in any Native American language. We do not separate things in this way. A piece of art is of no use other than its beauty, yet an artefact serves a function in the living of our lives, as well as being beautiful.

The last lesson that can be learned from the spider is patience. Once the web has been woven the spider does not go out and hunt for its food. It waits and waits, sometimes for days, until the web traps its dinner. There is more to its patience than this, though. Most of the weavers of these webs are female. They also have the patience to await the arrival of the male to do what is necessary for the continuation of the species. When he finally does arrive she will let him have his way with her, then, unless he's quick enough to escape, she will have him for dinner! Patience does have its limits.

There are lessons to be learned from everything that lives, but it is important to be realistic in the seeking of these lessons. Should you begin a search for teachers or totems to help you in your life, consider that there are important things for us to learn from in the least likely of places. Also, the lessons that we can learn from the more prominent or romantically attractive totems, such as the eagle or the bear, are not always what they seem.

In the instance of the eagle, many perceive the life of the eagle to be one of freedom. We would all like to be so free as to be able to take to the air and soar above the hard life that earthbound creatures must endure. Yet the eagle is one of the laziest of creatures; they only fly out of necessity. The term 'fed up' is a falconry term. Commonly, the definition of 'fed up' is to be annoyed or upset about a situation. The original meaning was to have a full stomach. If a bird of prey has a full stomach it is said to be 'fed up' and no amount of coaxing will get it to perform. It will just sit, not bothering to do any more than get out of reach of its handler. This is not the romantic lesson of freedom that the eagle brings to mind for a great number of people.

The bear is another totem animal that is only partially understood. There are accounts of the bear spirit aiding a person in returning to the earth or grounding. This is not untrue but the bear teaches much more. We can learn of survival from the bear. Should anyone have the opportunity to follow a bear in the wild they could learn of the things that can be harvested from nature that are capable of sustaining human life. The bear eats fish, and not just any fish, as a rule, but the best – salmon and trout. They also forage for berries; again, those that are also good to humans – blackberries, raspberries and blueberries – rather than those that would be harmful to us are preferred by the bear. In addition they get a great deal of their protein from grubs and insects that though socially unacceptable to us would in fact be good for our physical well-being.

Relationships with animals are also revealed through the legends of different peoples. In one story of creation told by a Cherokee, the spirits that were to come to live on earth were given a choice of what form they were to take. Among these spirits were six brothers. Five of the spirit brothers decided to become human but the sixth chose to become a bear. This is how the Cherokee came to regard the bear as one of the clans of their nation. They believe there are six clans whose origin is from the time of creation; five of them are human and the sixth is the bear – their brother in Spirit.

There is a tendency for humans to read human characteristics into animal behaviour. This is one of the reasons for our sometimes fanciful ideas about the lives of other creatures. We see the flight of an eagle as an expression of our concept of freedom. Some even interpret the facial expressions of our pets. In many ways this is a recognition of the 'Medicine' that I spoke of in Chapter 2. It is a form of spirit communication that takes place between the spirits of different species.

Totems on the Wheel

I am often asked to 'show' a Medicine Wheel to someone. Since the Medicine Wheel is the circle of life, this is rather difficult to accomplish. You see, every aspect of creation is a Medicine Wheel. The Medicine Wheel is the nucleus of an atom, something that we are far too large to even see; it is the universe, something that we are far too small to comprehend. It is also everything that exists between those two things. Each and every one of us is a Medicine Wheel made up of Medicine Wheels.

The same is true of the other members of creation. The difference between humans and all other living things is that they live in balance with others and within their individual Wheels. We don't. It is therefore up to each of us to find a balance within our own lives. This must be done by each individual but it does not have to be done without assistance. We all have helpers and teachers available to us that will guide us on the search for our own understanding and aid us in finding balance in our Wheel.

These helpers/teachers are the totems of our Wheel. In many cases we share common totems, but not always. The trick is learning to identify the totems that are yours, and why they are for you.

When I was a child my grandfather helped me to identify the animals that fit on to each of the directions of my Wheel by telling me about his, and about how the lessons that they taught guided him. In my advanced age I am no longer able to recall what his totems were, but I will try and help you find yours by telling you about mine.

East

When looking for the totem or teacher for any aspect of your Medicine Wheel you must examine whatever you can find out about the true life of the totem creature, as well as the idealistic image of it.

Recall the way that most people see the spider. Now consider the way of life of a spider and the benefit that can be drawn from gaining lessons from it. It is in this way that you need to look for your totems.

In the east I looked at the events that occur in the east of a day, year and lifetime. The common links between these events are the fact that they are beginnings, and a physical property that involves light. In the beginning of a day the sun rises and sheds light on our part of the earth allowing us to see. Our vision improves as the light from the sun becomes stronger as it rises further above the horizon. In the Spring of the year the plants come out of the darkness beneath the ground and reach for the light. They grow and mature visibly throughout the Spring and into the Summer. The infant leaves the darkness of the womb and comes out into the light, separating itself from being a physical part of the mother. Then it is able to develop its sight and be better seen by others.

Aside from the east of the Wheel being the direction in which to look for new beginnings, it is the direction that requires or needs clear vision. It is for this reason that my totem for the east is the eagle. Despite my earlier comments about the life of the eagle, it is, to me, the prime example of clear vision. When the eagle is on the hunt it flies the highest of all the birds and, apparently, sees the clearest. From a great height it is able to spot prey that we would have difficulty seeing if we were right on top of it.

The bald, or fish, eagle is my totem. Not only does it fly high but it sees so well that it can pick out a fish under the water from a great height. And not just any fish either; the bald eagle only goes for the best. With the help of the eagle I strive to gain the ability to step back and see clearly the goals I should aim for whenever I begin a new venture. With the eagle as my guide I strive to acquire only that which will do the most good in my ventures, hoping to avoid the skinny perch and the muddy carp.

South

In this direction I have found different totems throughout my life. It was not until I arrived in England that I came to a fuller understanding of the time of the south by becoming a father. I had lived through many a midday, not so many Summers, and only one childhood. After the birth of each of my sons I learned more and more about the power of the south by observing the innocence, curiosity and furtive activities of toddlers that lies within the power of this direction of the Wheel.

Many animals reflect examples of these powers but, for me, none as well as the mouse. If you consider the actions of the mouse you can see the actions of a toddler. The mouse curiously examines what it finds and moves on to the next with great speed. In addition they have an innocence that children (and many adults) also display. Consider the fact that there never seems to be just one mouse in your house, and that some must have observed the one that died in your trap. Yet the next time you set the trap there is going to be one that thinks to itself that getting caught in a trap is something that happens to others – 'not to me'.

West

You have probably already gathered that my totem animal for the west is the Thunderbird. However, as with all the directions, you should examine the animals or creatures that attract you personally in order to identify your own Wheel's parts. There could be a bear, or perhaps an owl or some other night creature that would give you the lessons you need to face the fear, overcome the tendency for destruction, and help you find the life gifts that are abundant within each of us.

North

In this last direction of the Wheel, again I have a mythical creature. This time it is a creature that I have discovered has a counterpart in ancient European cultures.

The power of the north is associated with wisdom and occurs at the time of the day and year that is, generally, related to rest and preparation. Therefore, the creature that comes to me is Waziri, the white giant that comes from the north each year and in its wisdom lays a blanket of white across the earth so that she may rest and prepare herself for the coming Spring.

This is what we do each night and in effect each year, as well as at other times in our lives. We pause and rest, reflect on what has occurred before, and prepare ourselves for what is to come. This is wise and a method of acquiring wisdom.

The European character that resembles Waziri is Jack Frost. I don't know a great deal about the origin of Jack Frost but his activity and the image of him reminds me of the white giant, even if there does seem to be little respect afforded to the European version.

Here, again, let me remind you not to just take and adopt my totems. Seek to identify the uniqueness of yourself and the reflection of that uniqueness that is revealed when your Medicine Wheel and its totems are found by you.

EXERCISE

Finding Your Connections

By now I hope you have begun to think in a way that makes the reality of the Medicine Wheel's existence in your life more obvious to you. It is therefore time to personalise your Wheel. As you begin this it is important to remember that what you find now will not always remain constant. Your Medicine Wheel, like life itself, is ever changing.

◆ Take a piece of paper and divide it into two columns. In one column make a list of the individual animals or creatures that you feel an attraction to. Begin by listing any animals that you may have for pets, and then follow with others that you have an affinity for, like pandas, deer, and so on.

◆ In the other column make a list of the creatures that repulse or frighten you. In this column many will list things like snakes, spiders, worms and slugs.

◆ Then, get yourself into a comfortable place and position, and with your lists at hand examine your feelings about each item. What is it about them that attracts you? What in their characteristics causes you to fear them or feel a sense of revulsion when you see or think about them?

◆ Once you have taken the time, and quite often it takes a long time, to identify the source or cause of your feelings, you will be more able to see a reflection of yourself. This reflection is a way of seeing the lessons that have been learned and have in turn become strengths. We also are able to find the lessons that need to be learned – the weakness within. Throughout our lives we are constantly in contact with the other aspects of creation, and this contact occurs on both levels of our existence – the seen and the unseen. The seen is the physical and we experience it through the senses of sight, sound, touch and hearing. The unseen is the Spirit and it is experienced through the senses that are often translated to be our emotions. In your search for the what and why of your attractions and repulsions you will need to break down the confusion that Western socialisation causes.

- When you have reached a clearer understanding of the reasons behind your likes and dislikes of the items on your lists, you should begin to examine the personal lessons that they are showing to you. One of the methods of clarifying these lessons is to do some research into the life of the creatures. Within the way a creature lives may be a lesson that you need to be aware of that will allow you to better understand yourself.

- Once you have begun to recognise the lessons that are available for you, it is time to find the direction of your Wheel that these lessons relate to. On a separate piece of paper draw the image of a Medicine Wheel. Now, keeping in mind the power, time and the circumstance of your life cycles, seek to match the teachers, lessons and the directions of your wheel. Once this is done you have begun to form a solid concept of your own personal Wheel and its totems. Look at it. How balanced is it? Where is it full? Where are there empty or weak spaces?

- If your Wheel is heavy or full of totems that are attractive to you in one direction, you have learned the lessons of that place and developed well. However, if there are aspects of fearsome or repulsive creatures anywhere (there should be), the lessons of that direction need to be worked on for balance.

The totems that have shown up are yours. Some of them are positive assertions of your strengths, others are those that you need to concentrate on to strengthen yourself through the lessons that they can teach you.

4

GIFTS AND GIVING

Through the years and events that have passed since the 'discovery' of the Americas by Christopher Columbus, there has been a drastic alteration in the peoples and cultures of the world. These changes have occurred as a result of the exchange of gifts that were held by the various different peoples involved. Through the passage of time, and the various methods of exchange and interpretations of events, the concept of what a gift is, along with respect for the gifts and the giving, have become difficult to recognise.

Many people hark back to 'the good old days', when life was lived at a slower pace and people seemed to present a keener awareness of their surroundings. People lived in communities, and activities that took place seemed to be supportive to the inhabitants of the areas where these communities existed. There was a visible system of exchange of goods and services that were needed by everyone. This held true throughout the world, within all cultures and societies. As time progressed there evolved greater contact between cultures and greater numbers and varieties of things were exchanged. These items of exchange were extremely diverse and included ideas, crafted (manufactured) goods, foods, beliefs and social practices.

As contact between the populations of the various communities of the world developed, the exchanges that took place became greater, and in many cases abusive. Over time, the origin of those things that allowed for the development of today's advanced, dominant cultures has been ignored. By ignoring the source of these gifts, such civilisations have increased their separation from their own foundations, as well as alienating, through disrespect and dishonour, the peoples that gave them a great deal of their power.

In Chapter 1 I spoke of the fact that Native Americans developed civilisations based on agriculture. Today, a great deal of emphasis is placed on the hazards of tobacco consumption, and there is a common practice of laying the blame for the use of tobacco on Native Americans because they were using it prior to the arrival of Europeans in North America. What should be recognised, however, is that it was a European (John Rolfe) who took a tobacco plant that was indigenous to another place and developed it into a cash crop. It is this that developed into the harmful abuse that causes so many health problems. The Natives' use of tobacco was much more temperate and therefore not so damaging.

Again, as discussed, the agricultural products of the Indian farmers were the foundation of a change in diet throughout Europe. This change led to a drastic improvement in the health of Europeans, and what followed was an extension of their life expectancy, drastic reductions in disease, and amazing developments in general lifestyle.

There is no doubt that the ships that sailed from European nations carried these foods from the 'New World' to Europe. The discrepancy lies in the assumption that the explorers 'discovered' these lands and the produce. All of the produce that helped to improve the lot of the disease-ridden peoples of Europe were products of Native American agricultural practices. Even the ships that sailed the seas were able to be built larger due to the acquisition of larger trees to make taller masts, a result of the land/forest management of Native America.

There exists a need for people to re-examine the source of the things that have enabled us to have a different life to that of our ancestors. Europeans and their descendants, the New Americans, should remember to honour and respect the peoples responsible for so many of the things that today's traditions are based on. This does not discredit the people that history has acclaimed as the innovators, explorers, pioneers and inventors. Credit should also be given to those that supplied the produce that made so much possible. The explorers did not find the new foods just growing wild in an uninhabited land, they received these things as gifts or as part of their exchange with an advanced, civilised people.

IMAGERY AND PHILOSOPHY

What did and still does occur in the various lands of the earth is a difference in the imagery, attitude and philosophies of the peoples that inhabit these lands. Europeans developed an attitude of superiority and a concept of living 'on' the earth, while the Natives of North America developed a sense of relationships and a concept of living 'with' the earth.

This difference is exemplified in the way that the island of Manhattan was acquired by the Dutch.

The colonial leader Peter Minuit saw a great advantage to be gained by establishing a colony on the island of Manhattan. This location had many points that would aid in establishing a strong foothold in this 'New World'. There was, at the southern tip of the island, access to the sea through deep waters, therefore large ships could enter this sheltered port. There was fertile land on which to grow crops. There was a good stand of timber that would provide fuel and building materials, as well as two rivers to give access for inland trade and exploration.

Peter met with the local natives and through negotiation gained permission to establish his town in their land. Part of the negotiations involved the Dutch leader presenting the native leaders with several boxes of trade items. These were things that were not common to the residents of this area, such as glass beads and metal tools.

At the end of their meeting Peter Minuit walked away, looking over this beautiful island and thinking how foolish the natives were to let him buy it for such a small price. On the other hand, the native leaders carried away the trade goods thinking, 'What beautiful things we have received to share with our people'. In their minds there was no idea of the transfer of ownership of the land; after all, how could you own or sell Mother Earth?

The idea of ownership of land was different for the Indians. Each Nation had their territory that was theirs to live in, as long as they fulfilled their responsibility to it. Land, 'Ina Maka' (Mother Earth), and all the other relations that lived within the boundaries of each Nation were regarded as being there to share life with. This gave no right of ownership in the European sense. There was no concept of domination and manipulation that leads to the destruction that is so common today. Rather, there was a sense of responsibility to manage the land and its inhabitants in such a way as to aid in the perpetuation of all living things. Helping to keep the balance so that all could share in the gift of life.

Plant Peoples

With this concept of caring for all the inhabitants of their area, Native Americans are further expanding on the concept of interrelationships that is expressed in *Mitakuye*

Oyasin. The life that is shared extends beyond the animal relations that I spoke of in Chapter 3; there is also a concept of a relationship with the plant peoples.

In the modern world there is a growing awareness of the significance of the plant peoples' contribution to our lives. Almost every day a protest group is trying to stop the commercial development of a green area, while more and more people are becoming involved in campaigns to stop the mass depletion of the rain forests in Brazil. Humans are beginning to see their relationship to the world's other peoples on a more personal level. This is a movement towards the way that Native Americans have traditionally viewed things.

In the course of the development of many Native American Nations, agriculture was based on 'the three sisters': corn (maize), beans (in many varieties) and squash (pumpkin and others). In other languages they were referred to by the same word as that used for 'life', because they meant the difference between life and starvation through the cold of Winter.

The close relationship between plants and humans is also demonstrated by the following Algonquian legend:

There came a time when the people had found a way to the land of the Creator that could be accomplished without death. It was, however, a very difficult path to follow and few had the courage to try. Three men were selected to make the journey and they set off together.

After many days through great hardships they finally

arrived at the land of the Creator. When the Creator became aware of their presence, it asked each of them what they would like to have as a reward for having come to this place.

The first man, who was very poor and had great difficulty in providing for his family, asked to be given the ability to be a good provider. He went on to ask that this gift be great enough to allow him to provide for the needs of anyone that he could be of help to.

The second man was disfigured and was shunned by many of the people of his village. He asked that his gift should be one that would give him the respect of others and cause them to seek him out to be of help to the people.

The third man was a very handsome man who spent a great portion of his day attending to his appearance. He wore only the finest clothes and was never seen in public unless finely dressed and groomed. He was also tall, but so vain that he stuffed his moccasins to make himself taller. His request was to be the tallest of all the people so that he would always be looked up to. Also, he requested to be given a very long life in which to enjoy his new status.

After hearing their requests the Creator gave each man a package that was sealed and bound with heavy twine. Along with the packages came instructions not to open them until they had arrived at their respective homes.

The men set off on their journey with great excitement and anticipation as to what the package that each had been given held.

When the first man finally reached home he immediately opened his package. His family watched in amazement as a cloud of beautiful smoke rose from the box and was breathed in by the man. He only had the sensation of smelling the most wonderful odour he had ever smelt. Before many days had passed, the people of his village began to notice that whenever he went out hunting he always brought home the finest game of all the hunters and in such abundance that he shared much with others in the village that were not so fortunate. As the years passed, many lived to thank this man for the wealth he shared so freely.

The second man arrived home to his empty house and had a similar experience when opening his package. Throughout the following months and years he displayed a new wisdom and understanding of the difficulties that arose in his life and in the lives of his neighbours and would advise solutions that worked. Soon he was sought for his counsel and given great respect throughout the land.

The third man was impatient to receive his gift and so stopped along the trail that lead to his home to open the package. He too was enveloped by a cloud of smoke that he inhaled, and he also received what he had asked for. In the time that it took to inhale the smoke his gift began to take form. His toes grew long and tore through his shoes at the same time as he began to grow taller. By the time he finished changing into what he had asked for he was over a hundred feet tall and his toes grew into the earth nearly the same amount that he stretched into the sky. His skin grew dark and rough and all his hair turned a beautiful green. Rooted into that spot beside the trail he became the first pine tree, looked up to by all, and he lived to a very old age.

This and many similar stories give evidence of the morality of the civilisations as well as the concept of *Mitakuye Oyasin* that pervades most, if not all, the Nations of Native America.

Another old legend that I have heard from several traditional sources tells of the day that all the animals held council. They were angry at the humans for killing their relations for food and clothing. The result of this council was that in retribution for the way we acted, the animals would give us illnesses and diseases to make our lives more difficult.

The plants heard of this and because they liked us decided to give us the gift of a cure for each ailment. It was left to us, though, to find which plant will cure or help with each ailment.

All of these things – the legends and stories, the way of life that is so close to nature, and the way of thought that recognises how we are so closely related to all life – gives the traditional Native American a purposeful existence that causes us to be ever aware of the need to live in as close a balance with the natural as we can.

This requires a lot of sacrifice and is not an easy way of life. It is far easier to destroy the balance by killing the creatures that cause you difficulties. Wouldn't the life of the shepherd and chicken farmer be easier and more profitable if there were no fox, wolf, coyote or weasel to deal with? In many areas of the earth this has come to be. The wolf and many of the weasel family are extinct or threatened with extinction. Protective measures have had to be put in place to allow whales and other sea creatures to remain in existence due to the overharvesting of the gifts of life from the sea. These are just examples of the result of an attitude of superiority and lack of responsibility.

THE EXCHANGE OF GIFTS

The way of life and the spiritual traditions of Native America (prior to the changes brought by modern civilisation) exemplified their attitude about their relationship with *Ina Maka* and *Mitakuye Oyasin*. Whether involved in the hunt, maintenance burning, planting/gathering of crops, fishing, cutting trees, or any of the other activities that were required for survival, there was some form of ceremony involved. I have heard many descriptions of thanks and honour given to the relation that has been required to give its life so that others may live.

These practices have often been misconstrued as multiple god worship. They are, in fact, a practice of a people that recognise only one Creator, but also the many gifts that are available through its act of creation. These gifts are no different from humans in the circle of life. They too have a spirit (soul) and are equally part of the web of life. When you recognise this and give them their due respect then your life becomes less harsh and more in balance. The act of recognition causes you to become more aware of your own actions, and through your awareness you become more respectful of the Creator and all the things that it gave the gift of life to.

Along with the gift of life itself the Creator gave each of us different skills to live our lives with. This is not just true for humans. All living things have aspects of their physical lives that are needed to be performed to help others to live well. Performing these skills is the way of the natural world; it is the act of exchanging gifts.

When the wolf pack takes its prey, the life of the pack is enhanced. At the same time a gift is given to others. In the first instance the animal that is taken reduces the numbers of its species. This prevents them from becoming overpopulated and ensures that their food source will not become so depleted as to cause starvation. Also, the pack will leave remains for scavengers to pick, and that which those scavengers leave will rot to provide sustenance for insects and the earth, thus helping with plant growth. This is a very intricate system that is considered a speciality of scientists today. In reality it is an example of the need for all of us to look at the effect we have on the balance of things. When farmers fence animals so they cannot defend themselves or run, they become too easy a prey. Then, as the most vicious of predators, we overcompensate by eliminating the other predators so our lives may be easier. This leaves us with an unnatural balance and our responsibility is increased.

THE GIFTS OF SPIRITS

All that I have spoken about thus far has to do with gifts in the realm of the physical. When considering the unseen or spirit side of things there are many more gifts to examine. There are the lessons that the lives of other beings can and have taught us, things that are relevant to our everyday lives that modern mankind is only now beginning to relearn and remember.

A great many people are aware of the ability of animals to communicate with humans. Some of it is fanciful, as in the case of the concept of the 'freedom of the eagle', other aspects are more real and the communication that takes place is interpreted in human terms.

Humans have also learned the right way of life from observation of animal behaviour and reactions (the source of the lesson is then promptly ignored once the skills are adopted). This is the case in the way that our modern society is structured. If you study the workings of a wolf pack you will see the prototype for human society.

When a member of the pack hunts for food they hunt not only for themselves but to feed the whole pack. Rabbits and other small game are passed by and the deer, elk, moose, cow or horse is sought. In bringing down such large prey they are able to provide for more of the pack.

We have institutions that we all support through taxation, charity, even lotteries, so that each of us contributes to the welfare of the human pack.

In selecting a mate, the Alpha male and Alpha female mate for life. We hold rituals that proclaim 'till death do us part' and methods of dissolution of our mating. The wolf does it and we play at it.

When children (cubs) are born the mother cares for them until they are weaned. In the pack there is a recognition that not all bearers of children are capable of teaching everything to their children. When the cubs are weaned their care and education is often relegated to another member of the pack. This member will then raise the cubs to adulthood, teaching them the skills and lessons they need to function as an adult. Is this not what we do when we send our children to school?

In village life among the Indian Nations all adults took the responsibility of educating all the children of the village. If a child wanted to learn a particular skill it would go to someone in the village that was proficient in that skill and ask to be taught. The teacher might be the child's parent, but not always. Each individual was recognised for their own particular gift and freely gave what they could in exchange for other things that they needed.

What is most important to learn here is that there are gifts that are both individual and collective – great gifts – and there is a need in today's world to honour those gifts. You could also say that all of life and all of our abilities are gifts. The purpose of any gift is for it to be given, or shared, and if this is not done the gift will be lost.

EXERCISE

Putting it All into Practice

As you have read through the previous chapters you have been presented with several suggestions that were intended to aid you in your awareness and development. Now is a good time to put several of these together so that you can see for yourself how these can be combined and adapted to your personal life.

♦ First, refresh your memory of the exercise 'Constructing Your Own Medicine Wheel' in Chapter 2, and perform this carefully. This time, however, you should concentrate on identifying your gifts. Look deep within and seek to name the things that you are good at. Some of you will find the list unimaginably long, while others will find it difficult to focus on more than one or two things. Do not be discouraged if you fall into the latter category. Many people have difficulty in accepting their own personal abilities.

♦ When you have completed your self-examination, return to the notebook that you started in the exercise in Chapter 2. Write down the gifts that you have identified and place them in order, with the one you consider to be the most important or strongest first.

♦ Next, consider the totem teachers that you felt an affinity to, in 'Finding Your Connections' in Chapter 3, and see how the lessons from your totem relate to your identified gifts. There should be some easy-to-see relationships between your gifts/abilities and your totems. If the relationships are not clear then re-evaluate your totems, gifts, or order of gifts by strength. There *will* be relationships that can be seen; sometimes it just takes a little practice to learn how to see them.

Once you have begun to recognise these relationships you have taken the first step towards honouring the source of your gifts, and by seeing how the connections are developed it becomes easier to translate that honour and respect into all aspects of your life, both in the spirit and in the physical. Next you will begin to recognise how your gifts grow and increase through your giving practices in everyday life.

5

TOOLS AND CEREMONIES

In every culture there are tools and ceremonies that are utilised by humans to aid us in our development and connections with others. Many of these tools are the same throughout the world. Some may be used in ways that appear different on the surface, or made up of different components; however, the differences are superficial and only lose apparent significance through individuals' lack of understanding or lack of respect for what they are doing or perceive others to be doing.

SMOKE

The use of smoke is one of the oldest and most documented tools in Spirit ceremonies. The differences in its use are superficial; the essence of its use is consistent throughout the world. Many people today use incense to alter the 'atmosphere' in a room or as an aid in meditation. And in many of the oldest practices of Christianity, frankincense or myrrh is burned to cleanse, purify and prepare people and an area so Spirit can work better through their ceremonies.

I would not attempt to explain how the use of smoke is understood in other traditions. I only know of it as being very important; important enough for burning substances to number two out of three of the gifts of the Magi to Christ. Also, important enough for the manufacture of incense sticks to be a major cottage industry in many Asian villages.

The use of smoke is also prevalent among Native Americans. Smudging with smoke is not just reserved for 'high mass', it is the prelude for virtually any attempt to work with Spirit. Smudging is a part of the ceremony of prayer, regardless of whether it is a ceremony of traditional foundation, like the *Inipi* (Sweatlodge), a healing ceremony for the ill, or a personal ceremony performed by a woman to help her through her Menses.

Different substances are used by people in accordance with the way they were taught and what is readily available when the need arises. Personally, I use sage; primarily white or desert sage when I am able to get it, but any sage is acceptable if harvested with proper respect.

EXERCISE

The Smudging Ceremony

In order for you to perform the part of a ceremony that involves smudging in the way that I do, you will need to acquire some objects. I always use an abalone shell to contain the fire or coal. You will also need some sage that has been gathered by hand so that the leaves are whole and dried on the plant stalk. The third item that I use is a feather or wing fan; the last item is a source of fire – matches or a lighter.

♦ Use the fire to light the sage, and when it begins to flame well softly blow it out so that it smoulders.

♦ After putting your source of fire aside, pick up the feather and turn to each of the four directions, using the feather to waft the smoke away from yourself. This will clear the path for whatever Spirit you will send through that direction.

♦ Next you should use the feather to waft the smoke over your head and methodically cleanse the whole of your energy field (aura) with the smoke.

♦ Now you are ready to continue with whatever ceremony you were preparing for. Set the sage in your shell so that it will be safe until it cools off.

Should you not have enough of a stalk of sage to hold without burning yourself then you could place the smouldering leaves in the shell during your cleansing. The holes in the shell should allow enough air through so that your fanning keeps the sage smoking. Also, should you need to you could use a piece of self-lighting charcoal in the shell and feed sage on to it (be careful of the bottom of the shell as it gets very hot under the charcoal).

Let me remind you that sage is what I use because I find it works well for me. Others use materials such as cedar, sweetgrass, juniper, lavender, and so on. Test out your own senses – find what works best for you.

The symbolism of the items used is also relevant to the Medicine Wheel and *Mitakuye Oyasin*. The shell gives respect to water – the life blood of Mother Earth. The plants that you burn honour the people that grow from the body of Mother Earth and fulfil many of our needs. The feather respects the air and the other two-legged creatures of creation, and the fire is symbolic of the cleansing fire of life itself.

CANNUMPA WAKAN

Cannumpa Wakan (*Chanoompa Wakan*) is the Lakota name for the Sacred Pipe, or Peace Pipe as it is commonly called. This too is related to smoke, but in a vastly different way than previously talked about. There are references to the Pipe in many books, as well as accounts of how we came to have the Pipe, and these are listed in the 'Further Reading' section. However, it is such an important tool in our culture that I must relate my understanding of it here.

In the days of the invasion of our lands there was much

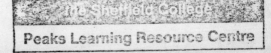

fighting and many treaties of peace were made. The invaders brought pieces of paper to our councils with markings on them that meant nothing to my ancestors. To these meetings the Natives brought the Pipe. Discussion took place and agreements were made. Further marks were made on the pieces of paper and the Pipe was smoked to seal the agreements.

All the parties involved left satisfied and confident that the agreements were binding. The invaders had made a treaty and signed what they perceived as a binding contract. The Natives left satisfied that the agreement was true and binding in the belief that whatever was said and agreed to over the Pipe must be true. It was their belief that no one could speak a lie in the presence of the Sacred Pipe.

It was through these meetings and treaties that the Pipe came to be called the Peace Pipe.

There are more significant and usual uses for the Sacred Pipe, however. It is a sacred object, the altar for the practice of our 'Medicine'; the altar for transmission of our prayers.

It would be improper for me to give you an account of how to use the Pipe in a ceremony in this book. It is important, though, for you to gain an understanding of the symbolism that is present in the use of the Pipe and to dispel some of the misunderstandings about its use.

To begin with, I have never, in all my fifty years, heard of the Pipe being used as an instrument with which to get 'high'. I have heard people talk about Native Americans smoking cannabis in the Pipe, yet none of those that I have heard were Native, nor did they have any concept of the culture of my people other than what they learned from Hollywood. The way of the majority of Native Americans did not involve mind-altering substances until we were introduced to alcohol. To use a Sacred object in such a way would have been against the teachings of the natural world.

The buffalo was a very important animal in the lives of my ancestors. They received nearly everything that was necessary for survival from this relation – food, tools, the walls of the home, blankets to keep warm with, even glue. They also received many lessons for their spirit from the life and spirit of the buffalo.

Cannabis can be found growing wild in the lands of my ancestors. The early stockmen known as cowboys called it Loco Weed; cows would go 'Loco' if they ate it. The buffalo avoid the cannabis when grazing. If a buffalo won't eat it, would a people that learn from the life and spirit of the buffalo be foolish enough to smoke it?

The symbolism of the Pipe should help you to understand its importance. The bowl itself is made of Pipestone, one of the rarest types of the flesh of Mother Earth. The stem of the Pipe is a piece of the standing people, the trees. Attached to the stem there will usually be found pieces of four-legged and two-legged relations that are significant to the Pipe carrier (the holder of the Pipe). When a Pipe is used, the hole in the bowl starts out empty, like the universe until it was filled by the Creator.

As the bowl is filled there are honours and prayers placed in it, along with the smoking plants, until it is full. Then the fire of life is added and the smoke that occurs is the visible breath of life that carries the prayers to where they need to be heard.

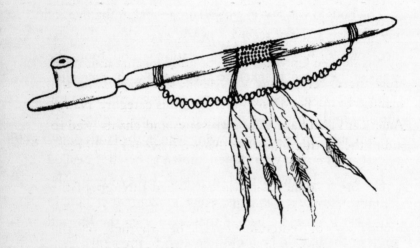

Should the opportunity arise for you to take part in a ceremony of the Pipe, or for you to acquire a Pipe of your own, this should give you a better understanding of the why and how of its use.

NOISEMAKERS

In order to aid and improve the connection to Spirit that people aspire to, the use of sound has been developed. Many instruments have evolved from this practice and are now used for enjoyable parodies of the original use of sound for Spirit ceremonies.

There are three primary tools still in use in cultures throughout the world: the voice, drum and rattle.

Everyone will be aware of the use of the voice. The hymns sung in Christian churches, the incantations cried from the towers calling the Muslims to prayer, and the mantras of the Buddhists all fall into this category. Native Americans also have their own songs and chants used to aid in the Spirit connection that we strive for in all ceremonies.

The use of drums has also developed throughout the world. In the modern 'civilisations' the drum is used as a foundation of entertainment. The rhythm of the drummer's beat is used to hold the focus of the musicians performing dance music.

The sound of the drum also performs another function. When the drum beat is heard the rhythm reaches into the emotions, feelings are aroused and bodies begin to sway, toes tap, anger is stirred, or peaceful feelings wash over the listeners. These are symptomatic of the use of the drum in Spirit Medicine.

In Native America the drum is also used in this way. At the Pow-Wows held all over North America the drum and voice are the primary tools used for the dance. Seldom is any other instrument made use of. At these events the singers assemble around a large drum and, usually, four men will beat time and lead the singing while others follow the beat with their bodies in dance. During such events a great deal of community Medicine takes place.

Another type of drum that is more widely used is the personal drum. These are small drums that vary greatly in style and shape. Some are made of hollowed logs, some have both ends sealed. The Natives of the plains have a personal drum that resembles the bodhrán of Eire.

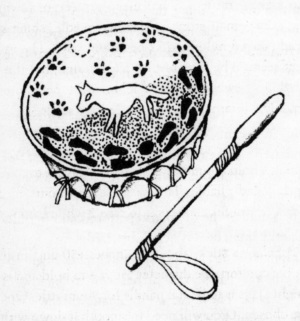

These types of drums are used by individuals in their personal ceremonial practices. When the drum is used the practitioner is attempting to refine their connection to Spirit. The beat is used to focus the physical and Spirit into harmony with *Mitakuye Oyasin*. The sound of the beating drum is the heartbeat of Mother Earth and, briefly, balance can be achieved when your heartbeat is in sync with the beat of the drum.

Rattles are used in much the same way as drums. The sound is vastly different and does not seem to resonate so deeply within us, yet it is a tool that is much easier to make and transport. Drums are readily available to purchase but rattles can be made easily by almost anyone.

To make a rattle you will need a piece of rawhide, a stick, some small stones, a leather needle, some strong thread (waxed nylon works best) and sand. The rawhide might seem to be the most difficult to find, but the large, tied dog chewbones available in most pet stores will generally contain enough rawhide for a rattle.

(1) Place the rawhide in water. If necessary, use a weight to hold it under the water and leave it to soak until it is soft and pliable. This takes several hours. I usually leave it overnight and go on to step 2 while I am waiting.

(2) Select a stick, about 12 inches (30 cm) in length, that is a comfortable diameter for you to hold and is fairly straight. This is to be the handle for your rattle. Once you have chosen it you will need to smooth it down with a file or some sandpaper (removing the bark if you desire).

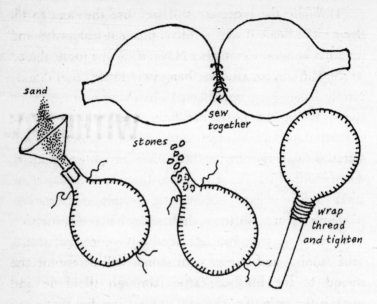

(3) When the rawhide is soft and pliable, remove it from the water and spread it out. You can now see how large a rattle you can make. Now, cut out two pieces of the same size, both roughly in the shape of a party balloon before it is blown up. When you cut the small end that protrudes from the main body of the shape, be sure that it is not wider than the diameter of the stick you have chosen. Once this is done you will need to sew the two pieces together using small overlocking stitches. It is best to do this in two stages: start from the top centre of the circle that is opposite the protrusion and sew around to where the protrusion breaks away from the circle. Then start at the same place again and sew it up in the same manner on the other side.

(4) While the hides are still wet, use the sand to fill your rattle. Pack it tight (with a poker if necessary) and create a balloon-like shape. Now, using the loose thread at the end of your stitches, hang your rattle up to dry.

(5) When the rattle has fully dried (this will take several days), empty the sand from it. Now you will need to submerge the tabs and open end in water again. This will not take long because the hide will now soak up water like a sponge. Be careful not to get it too wet. You only want to soften it slightly so that you can attach your rattle to your handle. Next, put your small stones (the number and size of your stones will determine the sound of the finished rattle) through the hole and stretch the hole over the end of your handle. Wrap and tie the tabs on to the handle. You can use string, thread, or even a thin strip of your rawhide. If you use rawhide you will need to soak it so it is soft and pliable.

(6) Lastly, hang your rattle by its handle until completely dry before adding whatever decorations you wish. Now you may use this very personal tool in any way that you need to aid you on your Spirit Path.

There are many other tools to aid individuals on their Spirit Path. The most important thing for you to remember is that the ones that are best for you can only be determined by you. Each individual must seek what works best for themselves, not be dictated to by others as to what is right. Make your own choices by following the feelings of your own heart.

INIPI AND INITI

As many people are becoming more aware of Native American traditions, so the Sweatlodge has been introduced. There are some who look upon this as a purely Native American ceremony. This is not true; the Sweatlodge was performed by virtually every tradition at some time in their ancestral past. The Roman Baths were born out of the Sweatlodge of the Mediterranean cultures; today's sauna comes from the Sweatlodge tradition of the Nordic peoples; and there were Celtic, Druidic and Pict Sweatlodges on the islands of Britain and Eire long before the Roman conquest.

In many Native American cultures the Sweatlodge is a very important ceremony. The form that this ceremony takes is as diverse as the many cultures that incorporate it in their tradition. Each leader of a lodge will perform the ceremony in a different way using the structure of ceremony that he or she was taught by their elders and led by Spirit to adapt to themselves.

The structure of a lodge in which a sweat is done is almost universally the same, however. Being ever conscious of the need for conservation, the framework is of willow or hazel, easy to bend, easily replaced, and from trees that are not destroyed by what is harvested from them. Long whips are woven into a framework that is similar to what is known in England as a bender. This framework is then covered with blankets or tarps to block out the light and for insulation.

This structure is considered to be the womb of the earth in the *Inipi* ceremony. What occurs inside is led by the Sweatlodge leader and is intended to aid in the physical and spiritual cleansing and rebirth of the participants. To tell you more would require greater detail than this work intends. Also, no one should make an attempt to perform a ceremony such as this without expert personal tutelage. The names of several Sweatlodge leaders are listed at the end of this book; their instruction should be sought rather than risking the danger of physical harm by trying this alone.

The *Initi* has existed for as long as the *Inipi*, but is considerably different. This sweat was performed much more frequently than the *Inipi*. Its purpose was for physical cleanliness. It was performed predominantly by the Natives of the plains and Southwest desert, where the scarcity of water caused them to bathe in the steam of a Sweatlodge. This practice was used extensively by women during their moon times.

The *Inipi* was done on its own or as a prelude to a more significant ceremony. The men and women that took part in the Sun Dance would first enter the *Inipi* in preparation. The same was true of those men and women going on a quest for vision, while the other significant use of the *Inipi* was for the child going through a puberty ceremony that would welcome them into adulthood at its conclusion.

All these tools and ceremonies are intended to be of help in living a more balanced life. They are the instruments of body and Spirit, and while acknowledged to be of Native American origin, they are no different, in essence, to all earth traditions. What makes them seem different is their outward appearance, and this is true of many aspects of the multitude of religions, societies and cultures throughout the human world.

6

SEEKING DIRECTION

Throughout mankind's existence there has been a need within individuals and groups to find for themselves a sense of direction through external guidance. This has been noted in the histories of most peoples of the earth. In fact, the religions of the world have many accounts of this search within the stories that they use to justify their beliefs. There have been many cases where this justification has led people to assume that the event of gaining guidance is reserved for only a select few. The assumption seems to be that those that receive guidance are unique, holy, special, chosen and separate from the rest of us.

Among the people of note that sought direction were Moses, Christ, Buddha, Merlin, Mohammed, John Smith and many others. These people then followed the guidance that was received. History has noted the significance of their lives because of the great effect they had on so many others, right up to the present day.

There is a need for all people to seek direction. In the Sixties there was a great movement within Western civilisation of people attempting 'to find themselves'. Today, one of the 'growth industries' is the field of personal development, reflected in the great number of training companies and organisations in existence. Everyone has an inherent need to find answers to help guide their lives.

In the tradition of Native Americans this act of seeking direction was/is a formal event available to each individual, one of the many ceremonies that each individual is presented with during their life. In Lakota it is the ceremony of Hanblecheyapi or crying for a vision.

SPIRIT VISION

In my youth, the terms 'dream' and 'vision' were taught to me as being synonyms. As they mean the same thing I had a difficult time in trying to establish how they could be looked upon as different by others. As I grew older and began to learn about the physiology of dreaming, it became clear that there are, indeed, two types of dreams. The first being the dream that the scientists recognise as those that can only occur during the sleep period. These are memory activations occurring as a result of the electromagnetic pulses that can be measured while you are in a state of sleep. As I understand it, stored memories are brought to a conscious level as a result of the electric pulses that pass through your brain during sleep.

This explains the many nonsensical dreams that I have heard people recount; they are just distorted memories of things that have recently occurred in their lives. It does not explain the prophetic dreams or the dreams that involve instances or events that have no foundation in the memory of the dreamer, however. It also does not explain the accounts of those who have experienced altered perceptions of their senses while awake; like the odour of a rose being smelt while walking on the moors in February; or coming face to face with a bear in broad daylight while sitting by a stream in Dorset.

The latter 'dreams' are commonly referred to as hallucinations, delusions, even insanity, particularly if they are followed by an alteration in the behaviour of someone that experiences such a phenomenon. These are not uncommon occurrences, though. The number of prophetic sightings that have preceded historical events are innumerable. One of the most significant examples was the sending of a telegraph to San Francisco warning of the great earthquake the day before it occurred.

A child's 'imaginary' friend is considered cute at first. Then as they grow older they are told to 'stop being silly', and comments are passed about an overactive imagination. This goes on until the child, like the adults around it, learns to be blind. The ability to 'see' and 'hear' things is, for most children, a natural ability that they are trained to ignore as they become older.

This alternate set of senses is celebrated in the tradition of Native Americans. Those that can retain the ability of 'vision' while not asleep are revered as having 'special' or sacred Medicine powers. These people are 'Wakan' – Holy.

Visions or altered senses that occur this way are Spirit Medicine. When Spirit is unable to communicate directly to the conscious mind it will convey its lessons through the dreams that occur during sleep. These dreams/visions are not the same as the memory dreams that scientists can measure. They are lessons that must be transmitted to the receiver, even if they refuse to accept them in their conscious, awake state. Visions that occur in this way should be recognised and understanding sought.

When a person has significant sleep dreams or enters into the ceremony of crying for a vision, and receives one, they may need a Wakan or Medicine Person to help them interpret their messages/lessons.

Crying for a Vision

Among various Native American groups, as well as individuals, there is debate about the way in which the Hanblecheyapi (vision quest) should be performed. There are several recorded accounts of the way in which Elders sought and received their visions. In a number of these accounts it is said that they were on their quests for four days. However, if people of today wish to follow the guide of an English version of an Elder's account, originally spoken in a language that does not translate directly word for word, several things should be considered.

Firstly, our Elders did not keep account of the passage of time in the same way as it is done today. The calendar used was one that followed the lunar and seasonal cycles and was therefore much more flexible. Also, my grandfather's concept of a day was the period of time between his sleep periods. There were many times that he considered it a new day after taking an afternoon nap, and in my dealings with several of my Elders/teachers I found this a common occurrence. Finally, when anyone enters an altered state and deals with Spirit they soon learn that time in the physical sense is suspended. The four days of a vision quest are the same as the six days of creation or the forty days of rain that flooded the world, or even the forty days of Moses and Christ in the wilderness. The way of the ceremony and the measure of time varies with the leader and participants involved.

There was no set age at which an individual was ready to seek vision. There were many that never took part in the vision quest and others that performed this ceremony a number of times in their lives. The most common time for someone to take their first vision quest was around the time of reaching maturity. It was then that the need for help in guiding their lives first arose.

Each individual that perceived a need to seek vision would approach a medicine man or woman and ask for their help. Should the Elder decide that they were willing to take on this responsibility they would then begin to instruct the seeker about the preparations that had to be made. Each culture, in fact each individual, would have different ways and different preparations.

In some instances, after their preparations were accomplished the seeker was taken out to an isolated spot and would dig a hole large enough to sit in and then be left with their items of personal Medicine, to pray (cry) for a vision. In other cultures this would take place in a cave or in the open atop a hill. The specifics of location would be determined by tradition and the place that the people inhabited on *Ina Maka*. The significant thing to remember is that the seeker was always isolated and the ceremony guided by an Elder.

Following the time of seeking, whatever might have been received would be recounted to the Elder and they would help to translate the vision and what it meant to the life of the seeker. It was through vision that many received their names or were given a gift of power. Many plant medicines were revealed through vision and many animal spirit teachers revealed themselves and taught their lessons through vision.

It was through vision that I received my name: Tsumanutu Tanka hota iyksija (Grey Wolf Stands Alone). It was not my own vision but the vision of an Elder who was told to pass it on to me. A name is a reflection of the person that carries it. The Elder that sent me my name had not seen me for some years, and received the new name for me during an *Inipi* ceremony. The meaning of it was unclear to him at the time but when he contacted me we soon understood its relevance. I am called 'Grey' due to having gone (prematurely) grey; 'Stands Alone' because I stand isolated from my people on this island (England); and 'Wolf' because of what I do – I teach about a way to live. Through the culture, beliefs and history of Native America my lessons have been of help to people of other cultures in finding their way back to the Mother Earth.

LIFE DIRECTION

There is another way to look at seeking direction that is used often by almost everyone. We pursue our direction through our 'intuition', 'feelings', 'conscience', 'sixth sense', and so on. Sometimes, people even rationalise this way of seeking direction by performing a ceremony that involves making a list of pros and cons relating to a difficult decision they are trying to arrive at. In making business decisions there is a formalising of direction seeking that involves bringing in analysts and other experts to aid in the process.

After all the deliberation, the end decision is arrived at as a result of what 'feels right'. In this form of seeking direction there is a tendency for women to have a distinct advantage over men.

Everyone is aware of the existence of 'woman's intuition'. This is the 'knowing' of what is the right way without needing proof, or even ability to explain how she 'knows'. Scientists have identified that women work with the right side of their brain, the side that is responsible for abstract thought and intuitive thinking. Men work with the left side, the side of the physical and rational, where there must be measurable proofs provided in order for something to be acceptable.

In the process of seeking direction women have, for a long time, been able to deal with the changes that life brings much more readily than men. As the Western world has moved further from the cycles of the natural world so there has been a movement away from recognising and seeking to develop intuitive abilities.

The cultures of Native Americans respected and sought the guidance that women have to offer. Despite the lack of recorded evidence, the Elders and leaders of many villages were women. We revered and respected our women as being equal to men. They were likely to have different gifts, but without their abilities everyone's life would be more difficult, and we would lose half or more of the wisdom that we needed to help us seek our direction.

TAKING THE NEXT STEP

The movement in the Sixties towards seeking an answer to the eternal questions 'who am I?' and 'what's it all about?', was undertaken with no foundation that could help those involved in their search for direction. The results were the development of a drug culture that failed, a number of disillusioned advocates for change with no concept of what the changes would result in, and many who returned to the established ways in frustration. This was a time when changes were needed but no means of seeking guidance was recognised.

The time has come again for drastic changes to occur. People are still looking for direction. This time, however, there is a massive swelling of people that are seeking to make more positive changes than in the previous attempt. This time they are not wandering aimlessly in search of themselves but seeking to re-establish a foundation on which to build a personal future. This foundation lies within the wisdom of the past and the peoples of the world that have maintained the tools that are needed; tools that are the essence of Native American, Australian Aboriginal, Celtic, African, Asian, and all other earth-based cultures; tools that help individuals and communities to live in closer contact with *Mitakuye Oyasin*. These tools are the ceremonies that honour the Mother Earth, aid contact through the Spirit of all of creation, and help in each individual's search for direction. They come in the form of stories, songs, teachings, ideas and senses that go beyond the physical and reach into the infinity that is the Creator of all that exists.

7

TOMORROW

Black Elk presented many lessons about the Medicine Wheel in the book *Black Elk Speaks*. Some were clear, others more elusive. As discussed in the Introduction, one of the most pertinent was that 'the hoop of the Nation is broken'. The way of life that had been theirs for so long was no longer possible. There are a great many individuals struggling with this 'broken hoop' in their lives today. The ways of the previous generations are no longer practical in today's world.

It is a nice dream to consider that we could go back to what are envisioned as the 'good old days'. However, we cannot return to the past. We must build a future using the past as our foundation. That leaves us with a need to repair the hoops so the future will be solid and will endure for the next generation. It would be wonderful if everyone could agree on where the breaks are and act in harmony to effect the repairs. This is not possible.

Everyone perceives things differently, so the way to repair the hoops of communities, Nations and the world will never be completely agreed upon.

In order for you to incorporate the idea of the Medicine Wheel into your consciousness you should be aware that you already use some aspects of circular thinking. When dealing with our conscience we all rationalise. For example, it is accepted that killing is wrong, yet the death of the plants and animals that we eat is considered acceptable. Good and bad, right and wrong are determined by the way that things occur and the reasons for their being done. They are not fixed concepts, but part of an ever-changing circle. The important thing is to increase your awareness of the way in which you live and to take into account the effect that your actions have on the cycles of the lives of *Mitakuye Oyasin*.

There is, in the Wheel, a process of understanding that gives recognition to the flow of life. There is no specific place of beginning and therefore no specific time for the changes that occur throughout the course of a lifetime. The Medicine Wheel is the circle of life and is different for each living entity. Each of us will find that the specifics that make up our understanding of the Wheel are different. It is the composite of the way that we each perceive the events that occur throughout the living of our unique, individual lives.

This uniqueness is the very thing that causes us so much difficulty. The breaking of the hoops of individuals happens as a result of our attempt to fit into a uniform, straight line concept of how things should be. We are incapable of all being alike and the Medicine Wheel celebrates the difference rather than criticising it. Each of us has our own gifts or abilities, and we each have our own limitations. When working to identify your Wheel it is important to recognise that not everyone is able to possess the same totems, colours or understandings. Each will have to search for the answer that best takes care of their needs. The old idea that there is one truth for everyone about any aspect of life must be put aside or you will fall into the trap of trying, and failing, to be someone that you are not.

It is also important to recognise the duality of the Wheel. I learned that 'all things are reflected'. In another tradition it is said 'as above, so below'. The Lord's prayer declares 'on earth so it is in heaven'. To me, all of these statements say the same thing.

Every tradition finds shapes in the stars that are reflections of things on the earth: lions (Leo), bears (Ursa Major and Minor), bulls (Taurus), even insects (Scorpio). These are just a sample of the reflections that are perceived. To take this further, I was taught that what a person sees in the world around them is a reflection of their own potential. If you only see harshness and cruelty in the world then you should examine the aspects of your life that are harsh and harmful to others. On the other hand, if you recognise the beauty of a butterfly, or the opening of a rosebud, then you are seeing your own potential beauty.

There is a ceremony that is practised by my people

called the Sun Dance. In the centre of the ceremonial circle a pole is placed for the dancers to be attached to. This pole is always forked. The fork in the pole stands out as a reminder of the fact that we are always at a fork in the road of life. No matter where we are on the circle of our lives, we are being presented with a choice of what we should do. In many respects this may seem very philosophical. It is, however, extremely basic and simple.

The idea of being faced with simple choices can be seen in the following example. A person comes to visit you and during the visit declares that they are hungry. Go into the kitchen, open a drawer and take out a knife. Now you must make a choice. You can use that knife to slice and butter a piece of bread so your guest will have their hunger relieved, or you can cut their throat so they will never feel hunger again. This is a drastically simple example that can be applied to every aspect of life. I used a hungry visitor but it could be applied to what to do with the empty sweet wrapper in your hand: will you drop it as litter or place it in a recycling bin?

This kind of consideration is inherent in the life of traditional Native Americans. The relationships that are recognised within the declaration *Mitakuye Oyasin* are translated into every aspect of life. The reflection that is found in the living example of a totem animal is the lesson needed to see how to live in a very practical way. There is a duality of the Spirit and the physical that needs to be recognised and balanced.

Looking at the image of a Medicine Wheel you will see

that there are intersecting lines running from east to west and north to south. These are the two roads that we have to travel in this life: the red road and the black road.

The black road is the road of the physical. This is the part of our life that we must deal with as long as we remain in this carcass that we call a body. It is the road that involves bank accounts, mortgages, electric bills, new cars, employment, and all the other chores that are required for life in this society. Should we choose to live solely on this road we are likely to have a miserable life. There never seems to be enough money to satisfy our wants. Just when we seem to have caught up and can relax, another bill comes in the post, or a newer, brighter gadget catches our eye. There is a never ending hunger for more, bigger, better and newer.

On the other hand, there is the red road. This is the road of Spirit, where everything is bliss. When you can get a firm footing on this path it feels wonderful. Everything is right, pain disappears, there is no hot or cold discomfort, there is no hunger as your spirit and body are filled with the elation of the sense of rightness. Yet your physical life would soon end if you were to stay on this road for any great length of time. After all, if you feel no hunger you will starve for lack of eating, and if you feel no pain or sense no danger you will lose the caution that keeps you from harm.

What must be developed is the ability to stand in the centre of the Wheel, keeping one foot on each road, holding yourself in balance; dealing with the physical as is necessary to live this life well, and dealing with the Spirit as much as is possible.

The lessons that are necessary to enable us to live in balance come from both roads. Throughout life we are presented with lessons in how to deal with the physical side of our lives. During infancy, the adults and older children around us give us these lessons. As we develop and grow the lessons are translated into our individual abilities. No one mimics exactly the physical skills that someone else teaches them. Physical differences and freedom of choice give us our individuality. That is how a left-handed child learns to tie a shoelace from a right-handed adult.

Just as physical skills and lifestyles vary, so does the spirit life of individuals vary. It is this individuality that is at the root of understanding and adopting the Medicine Wheel as a tool for living and understanding. No single teacher, physical or spirit, can teach anyone all that will be needed to fulfil any individual, however, the Wheel, when understood, incorporates all that is needed. The concept of the Wheel is a universal tool, but the reality of the circles and cycles of the Wheel are individually unique. You are a Medicine Wheel and therefore need to find the teachers and tools that will allow you to find your own centre and identify your position on your circle. You will then be able to learn the ways in which to seek the direction that will suit you and enable you to grow and develop in balance with the others that live alongside you in this life.

Just as the way of life of ancestral Native Americans was difficult, constantly fraught with the dangers that come with living in the natural world, so today's life is difficult. Developing your perceptions of your own Medicine Wheel does not stop these difficulties. What the Wheel will do is help you to identify your strengths, weaknesses, and how to seek the lessons necessary to overcome obstacles or accept limitations.

Until now you have learned about the circle as a level plane with four directions – east, south, west and north – in which to look for the lessons you will need. There are actually seven directions in which to look if you wish to find balance. The Wheel is more a gyroscope than a compass. The other directions to look are above, below and into the centre.

Recall that I spoke about *Ina Maka* (Mother Earth). She is the equivalent of our human mother when we were infants. All that we need to live is provided by her, and as we grow she teaches us to make use of what she provides for ourselves. She personally gives us lessons as well as presenting us with the teachers we need in order to improve our life. These teachers come in many forms, some of them being the totems that you learned about. Look down to seek the Mother; she is always there at our feet, the foundation of the physical life that we live.

Just as in our physical lives, the Mother is not the only provider. There is also the Father. The Father figure of the Medicine Wheel is found in the above direction. The Father is this entity that I have referred to as the

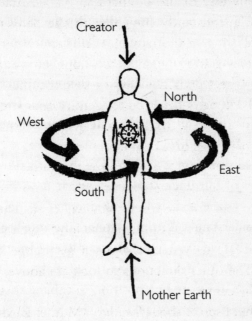

Creator. There are many terms used to identify this entity: Christians use the name 'God', Muslims 'Allah', and Jews 'Yahweh'. The translation credited to Native Americans is the 'Great Spirit'. While it is difficult to translate many terms into English from my ancestral language, the term Great Spirit is a reasonable interpretation. I feel that there is a more concise translation, however. The actual words in Lakota for the Creator are 'Wakan Tanka', a more accurate, direct translation of which would be 'Big Mystery'.

Whether you prescribe to a theory of creation or the scientific approach to explain the existence of the universe and life, you cannot deny the mystery of it. The Medicine Wheel is one tool that can be used to help understand the way of living in balance, but it does little to solve the mystery of the existence of life itself. The big bang theory is merely evidence of the occurrence of life and will never solve the mystery of its origin. The source of creation will be an eternal mystery to us as long as we are in this physical life.

The final direction is within. It is this direction that is the source of our understandings. What is within is the reflective surface that will show us what is, personally, ours to understand. Within is found the intersection of the roads that we need to balance our lives. Once an individual begins to develop a sense of balance in their personal life, they are in a position to expand their circle to encompass a larger area. In this way a personal, healing balance is able to spread from the centre of individuals to communities, and then onwards to aid the healing of the world.

FURTHER READING

As I can only guess what you would like to learn more about or receive personal help with, I have compiled a list of recommended books that fall into two categories: history and spirit/philosophy. These areas are so intertwined that when reading about them you may find that they cross so much as to be considered the same. Our history is the foundation of our present in Spirit.

BOOKS

History

Matthieson, Peter, *In The Spirit of Crazy Horse*, Harper Collins, 1992

Weatherford, Jack, *Native Roots*, Ballantine, 1991

Weatherford, Jack, *Indian Givers*, Ballantine, 1988

Wright, Ronald, *Stolen Continents*, Pimlico, 1992

Spirit/Philosophy

John (Fire) Lame Deer & Erdoes, Richard, *Lame Deer, Seeker of Visions*, Simon & Schuster, 1972

McGaa, Ed, *Mother Earth Spirituality*, Harper Collins, 1990

McGaa, Ed, *Rainbow Tribe*, Harper Collins, 1992

Neihardt, John G., *Black Elk Speaks*, University of Nebraska, 1995

Grey Wolf et al, *Earth Signs*, Rodale, 1998

Grey Wolf & Baggott, Andy, *The Friendship Pack*, Tuttle, 1999

PERIODICALS

Sacred Hoop Magazine
PO Box 16
Narbeth
Pembrokeshire SA67 8YG

Kindred Spirit Magazine
Foxhole, Dartington
Totnes
Devon TQ9 6EB
tel: 01803 866686
e-mail: editors@kindredspirit.co.uk
www.kindredspirit.co.uk
Published quarterly; £3 (UK)

USEFUL ADDRESSES

The following is a list of people and organisations that may be helpful to individuals seeking a life path that is closer to the tenets that this book has presented. There are many ways and tools that can help people find their own way. Those listed are all seekers who have found ways to help others. Each is valid, but all are not for everyone. Have a chat with them and decide if you feel that their way could help you.

Grey Wolf
71 Hambleton Drive
Halifax
West Yorkshire HX2 8TA
tel: 01422 240800
e-mail: tsumanitu@hotmail.com

Faculty for Shamanic Studies
Kenneth Meadows
Teaches the use of Shamanic tools and practices that can be of use to people in the modern world.
PO Box 300
Potters Bar
Hertfordshire EN6 4HW
tel: 0976 252499
e-mail: shamanics@aol.com

David Wendel-Berry
Wilderness earth-quest leader drawing on Celtic traditions.
1 Green Court
Kings Stanley
Stonehouse
Gloucestershire GL10 3QH
tel: 01453 828645
e-mail: david.wendl-berry@talk21.com

Grandmother Twillah Wolf Clan Teachings
Teachers from the Wolf Clan Teaching Lodge share the wisdom of living in wholeness, as taught by Twylla Hurd Nitsch, Seneca Elder and Philosopher.
tel: 01225 313032 (Anna Gahlin) or
tel: 01582 760434 (Janet Sleigh)

Scandinavian Centre for Shamanic Studies
Jonathan Horowitz and Annette Host
Shamanic teachings for a spiritual path.

Artillerivel 63/140
DK 2300
Copenhagen S
Denmark
tel: 0045 3254-2808
e-mail: ballon140@get2net.dk

UK contact:
Kathy Fried
tel: 020 8459 3028

Eagle's Wing
Leo Rutherford and Howard G. Charing
Courses and workshops on Shamanic healing and practices.
58 Westmere Road
London NW2 3RU
tel: 020 7435 8174
e-mail: eagleswing@shamanism.co.uk

INDEX

*Piatkus Guides, written by experts, combine background
information with practical exercises, and are designed to
change the way you live.
Titles include:*

African Wisdom   Owen Burnham

A comprehensive introduction to the spirituality
of the people of Africa. Meditations and rituals help
you bring the healing beauty and power of African
traditions into your life.

Angels   Paul Roland

Angels shows you the purpose and hierarchy of angels and how to
contact them and experience their love and advice. Find out how
our Guardian Angels protect us and how to ask for guidance and
inspiration.

Astrology   Carole Golder

Astrology is a fascinating introduction to the principles of
astrology with new insights into working with the positive and
negative aspects of your sign.

Celtic Wisdom   Andy Baggott

Celtic Wisdom is a dynamic introduction to this
increasingly popular subject. The author covers Celtic spirituality,
the wisdom of trees, animals and stones, ritual and ceremony and
much more.

Colour Healing   Pauline Wills

Colour Healing explains the vital role colour plays in your
physical, emotional and spiritual well-being and how it is used in
healing. Meditations and practical exercises will help you to
discover the vibrational energies of all the colours of the
rainbow.

Crystal Wisdom   Andy Baggott and Morningstar

Crystal Wisdom is a fascinating guide to the healing power of crystals. It details the history and most popular modern uses of crystals and vibrational healing. It also covers colour, sound and chakra healing, and gem, crystal and flower essences.

Druidry   Philip Shallcrass

Learn about the history and development of druidry, its divination methods and healing traditions. Discover how understanding the ancient wisdom of the druids can help unlock your creativity and inspiration.

Earth Mysteries   Paul Devereux

Earth Mysteries is an authoritative and easy-to-read analysis of the mysteries surrounding ancient sacred sites. It includes information on mysterious energies, sacred geometry and ley lines.

The Essential Nostradamus   Peter Lemesurier

The Essential Nostradamus charts the life of this extraordinary man, and includes newly discovered facts about his life and work. Peter Lemesurier unravels his prophecies for the coming decades.

Feng Shui   Jon Sandifer

Feng Shui introduces the origins, theory and practice of the Chinese art of perfect placement or geomancy. It provides easy-to-follow techniques to help you carry out your own readings and create an auspicious living space.

Kabbalah   Paul Roland

Kabbalah is an accessible guide to the origins, principles and beliefs of this mystical tradition. It includes original meditations and visualisations to help you gain higher awareness and understanding.

Maya Prophecy   Dr Ronald Bonewitz

Maya Prophecy is an intriguing introduction to the prophetic warnings for the future from one of the greatest early civilisations. It explores how Maya religion, mathematics and the Maya calendar provide support for the veracity of the prophecy, and how you should prepare for what lies ahead.

Meditation   Bill Anderton

Meditation covers the origins, theory and benefits of meditation. It includes over 30 meditations and provides all the advice you need to meditate successfully.

Native American Wisdom   Grey Wolf

A fascinating insight into Native American culture and the traditional ceremonies and tools used for spiritual healing. Discover the essential bond between ourselves and the spirit world.

Pendulum Dowsing   Cassandra Eason

Pendulum Dowsing is an accessible exploration of the history of dowsing and the techniques used to find lost objects, channel healing forces and tune into the psychic world.

Psychic Awareness   Cassandra Eason

Psychic Awareness is a fascinating guide to using the power of your mind to enhance your life. Simple exercises will develop your abilities in clairvoyance, telepathy, detecting ghosts, dowsing and communicating with a spirit guide.

Reiki   Penelope Quest

Reiki explains the background to this healing art and how it can improve your physical health and encourage personal and spiritual awareness and growth. Discover how simple Reiki is to use, whether for self-healing or treating other people.

Shamanism   Gordon MacLellan

Shamanism is a helpful introduction to the key concepts of shamanism and how to use them in your own life. Learn how these ancient powers for healing and creativity can be used in many modern situations.

Tarot   Cassandra Eason

Tarot's carefully graded advice enables readers to obtain excellent readings from Day One. You will quickly gain a thorough knowledge of both Major and Minor Arcanas and their symbolism, and learn how to use a variety of Tarot spreads.

Tibetan Buddhism   Stephen Hodge

Tibetan Buddhism explains the basic teachings and central concepts of Tibetan Buddhism. There is also guidance on basic meditation, the nature of offerings and worship, and the requirements for embarking on Tantric practice.

Piatkus Books

For the Very Best in Mind, Body and Spirit

We are a leading independent publisher, publishing 200 books a year. Our subject areas include fiction, health, mind, body and spirit, self-help, parenting, business, popular psychology, biography and history.

Check out our latest releases and bestsellers on our website at

www.piatkus.co.uk

Or write to us for further information and a catalogue with our complete list of titles:

Piatkus Books
5 Windmill Street
London
W1P 1HF

Tel: 020 7631 0710

Email: info@piatkus.co.uk